Follow
the
Yellow
Brick
Road

See what others have to say about this book:

"Your book, *Follow the Yellow Brick Road,* is a wonderful metaphor for understanding our lives and our relationships. I would recommend it to anyone as a tool for personal or corporate growth."

Dan Maltby, Ph.D., Director of the M.A. Degree Program in Organizational Leadership, Biola University.

"Personal growth is one of the most important tasks we can undertake in life. Dr. Alibrando's skillful use of the beloved Wizard of Oz tale as a paradigm helps instruct and guide us toward growth and change, in a warm and safe way. Change and transformation are understandable and attainable, as the book teaches us.

Dr. John Townsend, radio talk-show host and best-selling author, including *Boundaries*

"In the creative use of a much beloved children's story, Dr. Alibrando opens up a whole new way of understanding interpersonal relationships. The allegorical use of Dorothy's three companions is both moving and motivating. Being successful in interpersonal relationships is becoming increasingly challenging in this age of disconnection, so I find the book both inspiring and illuminating–a sort of 'Pilgrim's Progress' for those who struggle to build meaningful relationships."

Archibald D. Hart, Ph.D., FPPR. Dean Emeritus, Graduate School of Psychology, Fuller Theological Seminary, and author of *Unmasking Male Depression.*

"Dr. Alibrando's unique use of characters from a renowned children's story provides simple, yet effective insights into how we … react to the world around us, and sets the stage for effective change and success in accomplishing the goals we've set for ourselves."

Robin Cornwall, Business Analyst, *USC Business Expansion Network*

"Dr. Alibrando leads us on a fantastic inner journey through our personal Land of Oz, using The Scarecrow, The Tin Man, and The Lion to represent three facets of our inner character. He deftly informs us about ourselves, explaining the five practices necessary for people to change."

Diane Tegarden, Author *Getting Out of Limbo: A Self-Help Divorce Book for Women*

"Through the use of this classic allegory, Dr. Alibrando explores the many facets of the human personality and proposes a clear and practical model for change. Accessible and reassuring, *Follow the Yellow Brick Road* provides valuable tools for self-assessment, understanding and positive growth."

Marion MacKenzie Pyle
Writer, Producer and Cable TV Host

"Who doesn't yearn to discover 'somewhere over the rainbow?' In his intriguing and insightful book, Sam Alibrando cleverly brings psychological concepts together with metaphors from the Land of Oz, giving the reader courage to stay on the path and follow their unique Yellow Brick Road journey that leads to enlightening truth, significant change and personal growth."

Judy Balswick, Ph.D., author of *The Family*, *Authentic Sexuality* and *Relationship Empowering Parenting*.

"Dr. Alibrando has written an important book. He helps us to discover ourselves in the familiar Tin Man, Scarecrow or Lion. His intuitive understanding of the mind answers questions we don't even know to ask."

Steve Julian, Public Radio Journalist and Host"

You can't fix what you don't understand. Dr. Alibrando elegantly takes the reader on a journey of life's problems and possibilities. He has presented timeless concepts for a life well lived. *Follow the Yellow Brick Road* is a beautiful piece of work and has made a contribution to all of us who care about human development. It was a pleasure to read.

Pat Murray, President of J. P. Murray and Assocs.
(Leadership and Team Strategies Expert)

Follow the Yellow Brick Road

How to Change for the Better When Life Gives You its Worst

DR. SAM ALIBRANDO

iUniverse, Inc.
New York Lincoln Shanghai

Follow the Yellow Brick Road
How to Change for the Better
When Life Gives You its Worst

Copyright © 2007 by Dr. Sam Alibrando

iUniverse books may be ordered through booksellers or by contacting:

iUniverse
2021 Pine Lake Road, Suite 100
Lincoln, NE 68512
www.iuniverse.com
1-800-Authors (1-800-288-4677)

The views expressed in this work are solely those of the author and do not necessarily reflect the views of the publisher, and the publisher hereby disclaims any responsibility for them.

ISBN-13: 978-0-595-42285-2 (pbk)
ISBN-13: 978-0-595-86622-9 (ebk)
ISBN-10: 0-595-42285-3 (pbk)
ISBN-10: 0-595-86622-0 (ebk)

Printed in the United States of America

Contents

Preface

I am pleased to present the third edition of my book. It was my intention from the first printing to revise and rewrite this book. My intention is fulfilled in this edition. I believe that it is a better book for the effort.

Please note that I changed the original subtitle, *Five Disciplines of People Who Actually Change*. I found this title too academic. My intention is to touch people where they live. Life is both wonderful and difficult. In order for it to be more of the former (wonderful) we need to learn how to grow from the latter (difficult). If reality has ever picked up your house – a metaphor for your life – and dropped it in a strange land, this book is for you. The principles in this book are universal and adaptable. Therefore it does not matter what your specific twisters involve – challenges in your role as leader, a harmful addiction, a relational problem, grief over a significant loss, or negative self-esteem – the practices of the *Yellow Brick Road* are as much for you as they were for Dorothy. In this spirit I have changed the subtitle to *How to Change for the Better When Life Gives You its Worst*.

Another change from the first two editions comes from the realization that Dorothy's journey on the Yellow Brick Road is the *Hero's Journey*. Whether or not L. Frank Baum knew it, he wrote the classic story of the *hero's journey*. I will discuss this in more detail in chapters following. Suffice it to say for now, however, that any of us who willfully (or unwillingly) cross the hero's threshold to face our greatest weaknesses and meet our most trying challenges with honesty and courage will also follow the journey of the hero.

If you read no other chapter in this book, please read the fourth chapter on Scarecrow, Tin Man and Lion. It is the centerpiece of this book. In it I present an interpersonal model that I developed over many years, drawing on the brilliant work of two psychoanalytic giants: Karen Horney and Wilfred Bion. Dorothy's three companions make this model friendly and memorable. It fact it was my use of Scarecrow, Tin Man and Lion to illustrate the model that lead me to recognize the many lessons of positive change contained in the Wizard of Oz story.

I would like to acknowledge L. Frank Baum, who over a century ago wrote the children's story, *The Wonderful Wizard of Oz*, that was to become a true American myth. It has inspired many media and intellectual ventures, most notably the beloved 1939 movie adaptation that most of us watched as children on network TV and since have in our DVD collection. The film, *The Wizard of Oz,* has become an American classic. For over sixty years, people of all ages have enjoyed this cultural gem of a movie.[1] It is widely believed that more people have seen the 1939 film of the *Wizard of Oz* than any other movie in motion picture history.

Baum's life was a veritable trip in the Land of Oz. He was a dreamer who started and finished more ventures than all but a handful of his peers. To mention only a few, he was an actor, theater owner, newspaperman, storekeeper, businessman, traveling salesman, stamp collector, moviemaker, and even raised and bred exotic chickens. He failed at almost everything he tried, except one. Baum was a consummate storyteller. He loved to tell tales, especially to his four children and to their neighborhood friends.

Baum found his long-awaited success when he wrote his first book, *Mother Goose in Prose* (1897) and the soon to follow, *Father Goose, His Book* (1899). But it was his third book, published in 1900, about a young girl named Dorothy, that engraved his name in history.

---

1. Unless otherwise specified, when I mention *The Wizard of Oz,* I am referring to the 1939 movie version of the book, since it is more familiar to people. When I do mention examples from the book (originally named *The Wonderful Wizard of Oz*) or differences between the book and the movie, I will note it in the text or in a footnote.

In many ways Baum's life paralleled the very story he told of Dorothy. He himself had to face many hardships and frustrations – twisters that brought continual upheaval to his life. No one would ever have heard of Frank Baum had it not been for his wife Mod (his Toto), who was a loyal friend throughout his rough journey and pulled back a few curtains on the many wizards that derailed him. We would not have had his wonderful story of Dorothy were it not for his mother-in-law, Matilda Gage (his very own Glinda), who directed and encouraged him to write down the stories that he told to the local children. Baum eventually found his courage, heart and mind as an author and has blessed us all for it.

A brief word about confidentiality is in order. Much of what I convey comes in part from almost thirty years of working with people in psychotherapy, as an organizational consultant and as an instructor in graduate school. I frequently illustrate my points by using examples derived from these real people and situations. However, I go out of my way to change the names and descriptions of the people to hide any and all identities. I often blend two or three people or situations into one example. Any similarity to someone you may know is not intentional and is coincidental.

I want to thank my beloved wife for being my supportive Toto. Her patience and support has been invaluable. I would like to acknowledge all my clients – both clinical and consulting. I have learned more about psychotherapy, consulting and living from my clients than from any psychology course that I have ever taken. Their courage to go through the growth process – to embark on the hero's journey: to leave old ways of thinking and face their weaknesses and challenges, is by definition heroic and the very essence of following the Yellow Brick Road.

I would like to thank Robin Cornwall for his encouragement to write the book in the first place. I acknowledge Mike Manning's major contribution to launching the first two editions. I would like to thank Karen McChrystal for her professional and affable help in getting this third edition of the book to you. And I want to applaud Barbara Kosoff's brilliant art work, which is now the cover of this book.

I want to acknowledge the contribution of Dr. Alan Hedman. In our current collaboration on a leadership application of my model, he has helped me refine several of the concepts in previous editions and added the *Hedman touch* to a several paragraphs in this edition.

And for dozens of others who have given me feedback and support through this entire process – you know who you are – I thank you.

I hope that you can benefit from the ideas this book presents. It examines the most basic of our mutual human experiences and frames them in the context of a marvelous story, *The Wizard of Oz*. It is my intent that it serve you as a guide to finding the way along **your** *Yellow Brick Road*.

1. Positive Change

SOMEWHERE OVER THE RAINBOW

I shall be telling this with a sigh

Somewhere ages and ages hence:

Two roads diverged in a wood, and I –

I took the one less traveled by,

And that has made all the difference.

Robert Frost, *The Road Not Taken*

Dorothy is about to take a journey on a road less traveled, one made of yellow bricks. And for Dorothy, that road *will* make all the difference.

Do you remember Dorothy? She is a young girl who lives on a farm in Kansas. One fateful day a twister comes through and lifts her small farmhouse up into the air, carrying both Dorothy and her faithful dog, Toto, to an unusual land. In this land, she begins a journey to the Emerald City where the Great Wizard of Oz lives. She hopes this great wizard will help her return to Kansas and to her Aunt Em and Uncle Henry. She is advised by a good witch to travel to the Emerald City by means of the Yellow Brick Road.

Along this road, she meets three companions: Scarecrow, who is looking for a brain; Tin Man in search of a heart; and Lion, seeking courage.

Together, they travel to reach the Wizard of Oz, whom they believe will grant their deepest wishes.

Along this Yellow Brick Road, Dorothy, her three companions and Toto have many adventures. When they finally reach the Emerald City and have an audience with the Wizard, they are commissioned by him to confront the evil Wicked Witch of the West. This quest is fraught with danger but eventually ends in success. When they return to the Emerald City, they discover that this great wizard is neither great nor a wizard: He is a fraud. However, the three companions realize that that the things that have been seeking have been fulfilled by the journey itself. Scarecrow realizes his ability to think, Tin Man fulfills his capacity to love and Lion proves his courage. And after much difficulty, Dorothy – through power that she always had – is eventually able to return home. However, she returns home a changed person – changed because she has traveled along the Yellow Brick Road.

As a psychologist who has helped clinical and corporate clients change for almost three decades, I have come to see this tale, *The Wizard of Oz*, as more than just an enchanting fable. I see it as a story of how people change. The process of growth often starts with adversity – any of the many twisters that life sends our way. And it ends in growth and prosperity because of the principles practiced by Dorothy and any of us who dare to follow her path.

Dorothy's journey on the Yellow Brick Road is the Hero's Journey, but here, the hero is a heroine and a child. No less heroic for being a child, Dorothy leaves the known Land of Kansas and crosses the hero's threshold into an unknown place where she faces many challenges. If she successfully confronts these challenges she will emerge stronger and more integrated. She will return to her home with a renewed self.[2]

Any of us who willingly – or unwillingly for that matter – cross that threshold and face our greatest weaknesses and challenges, with honesty and courage, likewise follow the path of the hero.

---

2. The reader is referred to the work of Joseph Campbell, if you are interested in finding out more about the hero's journey.

The hero's journey turns adversity into growth. This is the hero's journey and the road the hero takes is paved with yellow brick.

From this classic story of Dorothy and her companions come powerful lessons in showing us how we can turn adversity into positive change and growth.

Dorothy's Journey

Dorothy is stuck in Kansas. In the 1939 film, nothing is terribly wrong with her life, but she is bored and lonely. She longs for "somewhere over the rainbow," for something more – a wish she is soon to realize. However, in the book, Dorothy's Kansas is bleak, devoid of any life and color, depressing. It is a cruel place to live by any standard. There is no thought of a rainbow, only grim existence. However, a twister is about to change all that.

As so often is the case, change does not take place in a vacuum but is rather a response to a life event. Dorothy's life-changing event is nothing less than a natural catastrophe that literally lifts her meager one-room house into another world.[3]

Dorothy arrives in a strange land, a colorful land, a land of danger and a land in which she is about to grow up. The film emphasizes the fact that Dorothy's journey is merely about gratitude, about realizing that "there's no place like home." However, Baum's book does not reflect this same kind of sentimentality. Dorothy's journey to the Land of Oz is not about appreciation but about transformation.

By the end of her journey, Dorothy has finished her work in the Land of Oz and is to return home. In the film, Dorothy never really visits Oz: She has simply had a dream. However, in the book, it is not a dream at

---

3. In the book, Dorothy, her Aunt and her Uncle live in a one-room farmhouse with a tornado cellar underneath. When the twister is about to hit, Aunt Em is so frightened and self-absorbed she hides in the cellar and locks Dorothy out to suffer the tornado on her own.

all. Dorothy's experience has been real, and by magic, she returns to Kansas a significant time later. She returns to a rebuilt house in Kansas, an improvement over the family's previous one-room farmhouse. This is noteworthy. When we successfully go through an Oz experience ourselves, inevitably the new home base that we form, personally or interpersonally, is almost always better and improved. This is the hero's journey, this is how we grow and change.

Your Own Journey

There are at least two reasons why people embark on the hero's journey. The first motivation is similar to Dorothy's in the 1939 film: a desire for something more, "somewhere over the rainbow." Human beings are by nature oriented toward growth. I call this type of motivation for change *alpha*.

There is a part of most of us that is internally driven to change, not because there is something wrong, but because there is something right.

It is the part of us that is spiritually minded and health conscious. However, with all the anxiety and stresses of life, this is not typically our main motivation. For most of us – myself included – it is the road less traveled.

The book version of Dorothy represents the second, more common type of motivation for embarking on the hero's journey. We embark on the Yellow Brick Road because our external circumstances (or inner pain) became too difficult to live with. I refer to this type of motivation as *beta*. *Beta-motivated* people do not think about change until there is pain and adversity. It is when our situation is so unpleasant or distressing we are *externally* driven to change. Any number of life experiences can generate this type of motivation: a divorce, a harmful addiction, depression, life-threatening illness, painful self-image, a midlife crisis or death of a parent. At work it could be low sales, partners not getting along with each other, an angry boss or board, negative morale, or massive restructuring.[4]

Most of the formative times of change in our life take place when we are children. Our brains are "ready" to learn when we are young; then the brain eventually settles down in early adulthood. We still can change in adulthood albeit with much more difficulty. However, there are certain times when we are more primed to learn, even as adults. Those times are when twisters pick up our house and toss us into another state. These times of pain, struggle, adversity and arousal are also times when we are more positioned to learn new life lessons – really and truly learn new things. So if you are going through a difficult challenge in your life, there is a silver lining. A road is open for growth and change. You can tell this road: it is the road less traveled and is made of yellow bricks.

This book is especially dedicated to people going through some sort of adversity. We all face difficult challenges every day and at some time or another we will all confront major life challenges (e.g. death of a loved one, physical illness, divorce, failure at work and inevitably our own death). There are two general ways to handle these life twisters, the healthy way or the unhealthy way. If we deal with these unavoidable problems the healthy way – which is often more difficult at first – we will get a double-benefit. First we will get through the challenge with the least amount of trouble. Most often the most productive way get through a problem is to honestly go through it, rather than avoid it. But there is also a second benefit of choosing the healthy way through a problem: we will also grow and change from the experience. Dorothy went through her remarkable life challenge with courage and integrity. Because of this she comes out of her experience with life lessons deeply learned. The same is true for us. However, it is often tempting to take short cuts and avoid the difficulties through less-than-healthy behaviors.

---

4. There are some people, regardless of how bleak their life is, regardless of how strong the tornado, will not and do not change. I refer to this type of motivation as *omega* – the last letter in the Greek alphabet. In other words, change is the last thing that they will do. They resist change regardless of the emotional, financial and spiritual consequences. This book is not for them.

In these cases we not only cause more problems later on but we do not learn and grow from the experience. Instead we become stuck.

People who do not change are stuck

Whatever your motivation, alpha or beta, if you join Dorothy on the Yellow Brick Road you will change … for the better. If you take the hero's journey, you will enjoy the hero's reward. However, if you do not choose the Yellow Brick Road, you will remain stuck.

Here are some examples of people who were stuck in their own Kansas:

> Jana was a talented upper-level manager. As an MBA from a prestigious business school, she knew the business side of her work inside and out. She had innovative ideas born out of thorough research and business savvy. However, she just could not get along with people. She treated support staff with contempt and impatience. Highly suspicious of her supervisors, she became enraged if they did not immediately recognize her ideas and achievements. Her peers could not stand working with her. In terms of her professional life, Jana was stuck.

> Jim, the pastor of a very popular church, was very well liked and charming. But Jim was trapped in an addiction to pornography. Whenever he was alone at home or sometimes at the church office, he would log onto Internet pornography sites for hours. This was incongruent with his values and notably interfered with his work and marriage. Jim's feelings became numb. Jim was stuck.

> Debbie was married to Joe for over ten years. She married Joe as a teenager in an effort to escape a controlling parent. The problem was that Joe was also a controlling person, insist-

ing on having his way and becoming enraged if she did not go along with him. Debbie learned very quickly to comply with his wishes. She complained to her friends, her rabbi and her relatives and even left Joe twice. But she quickly came back into the relationship, because Debbie was stuck.

John loved his children. There was little he would not give them – except his time and his patience. When he was not around the children, he would think of them fondly and proudly talk to others about them. But not long after he was around them, they would start to "get under his skin" and he would become agitated and highly critical of everything and anything that they would do. John knew that he was overreacting, but he was stuck.

In each of the above examples – whether it pertains to effectiveness in one's career, compulsive behaviors, personal relationships or parenting – someone is stuck in a significant way.

I remember sitting in a large conference room during my first internship. About twenty of us were grouped around a table with a consultant sitting at the head. A fellow intern presented the case of a woman who was being physically and emotionally abused by her alcoholic husband. How sad, I thought. The consultant asked for any other pertinent information from the woman's history. It was her third marriage and the two previous husbands were also abusive and alcoholic.

"What about her childhood?" asked the consultant.

It turned out her father was – you guessed it – abusive and an alcoholic. I remember how stunned I was by this. This woman was moving from relationship to relationship with persons of the same type. As a new intern, I could not believe what I was hearing. This woman did not change. Many people, in ways big and small, become stuck in their own kind of bleak Kansas.

This kind of pattern can be seen in the business world. Executives within an organization often establish modes of leadership and management that to outsiders are obviously negative and dysfunctional.

But often these same executives are not able to admit that how they treat people or lead is ineffective if not downright destructive to morale, motivation and eventually to the bottom line.

Results of Not Changing

Every potential hero has the opportunity to go back, to return to the familiar. If Dorothy did not go the distance on the Yellow Brick Road, she would have gone back to Kansas UNCHANGED. She would not have grown. The results of not growing or changing are many faceted. Here are six common consequences resulting from an inability to change.

Negative effect on love and work

Sigmund Freud once suggested that the essence of life is love and work. Much of who we are can be put under one of these two general categories. Love includes our intimate relationships, family life, dating and partnering, our passions and charity, our work relationships and team-building capacity. Love is how we relate.

Work involves our efforts, activities and creations. It includes how we earn our living, parent our children, keep house, develop and keep a career, engage in our hobbies. Work is what we do.

What I have noticed over and over again in my clients – both business and clinical – is that when they get involved in the positive process of change, their love and work capacities both improve. Their relationships become healthier and they achieve more success in their work. People who do not grow and change remain stagnant or even diminish in their ability to love or work.

High cost of maintenance

It actually takes more psychological energy to *not* change than to change! Freud first introduced the term "defenses" and "resistance," both of which convey the idea that human beings subconsciously "try" to keep things the same, to stay in Kansas at all costs. Remaining the same requires tremendous psychological energy and cost. We are not always aware of the toll it takes in terms of:

- Physical tiredness, exhaustion, fatigue, lack of energy and motivation
- Physical illness, somatic symptoms, neck aches, back aches
- Tension, anxiety, sleep and eating problems
- Poor decision-making, mistakes and even accidents
- Fiscal problems, impulse buying, bad business decisions, low productivity
- Relational stress and dysfunction, family and work conflict

Reality

People who do not change prefer to create their own reality. They have to create their own reality because life is always challenging and demanding us to accommodate, learn and grow. If people do not change, they are not respecting reality. To avoid change, they create and live in an "alternate reality."

In the movie called *A Man with Two Brains*, Steve Martin plays a widower who has met a femme fatale. At one point, he stands in his living room before a portrait of his deceased wife, asking her, by some ghostly intervention, to give him a "sign" if she thinks that he shouldn't get involved with this temptress. There is a sudden explosion with great chaos and turmoil: Household items are hurled through the room, and the deceased wife's picture starts turning around on the wall. The fracas finally settles, and Martin, with that inimitable unruffled composure of his, says, "Just *one* little sign." He obviously isn't responding to reality.

All the signs are there – he is just choosing not to respond to them. He does not want to change his mind. He does not want to change.

Maturity

People who do not change tend to be more immature than people who *do* change. This is understandable. Again, if learning how to live in reality defines maturity, then people who do not learn, or change, will be less developed. They will be more selfish and have less depth than someone tutored by reality. I've had many adult clients who describe a parent who behaves in childish ways, being remarkably self-centered and at times even throwing a temper tantrum. It is reasonable to assume that these parents have not consistently and successfully traveled the Yellow Brick Road but instead insisted on staying the same. Any chance to take the hero's journey would be summarily dismissed.

When we first meet Dorothy, she is in early adolescence. Adolescence is a time of tremendous change and emotional turbulence; it is the transition from childhood to adulthood, from immaturity to maturity. If Dorothy failed on her journey on the Yellow Brick Road, she would have still grown physically and intellectually, but she would not have grown psychologically. She would have avoided what reality had to teach her and stayed emotionally young.

Going the way of the dinosaur

People who do not change usually do not adapt either. We are fairly certain that the dinosaurs disappeared due to a catastrophic global event. Unlike other living creatures that are still here today, they were not able to adapt to the change. This principle is certainly true in the business world: Horses turn into cars, typewriters give way to computers, and blacksmiths and typewriter manufacturers go out of business. People who conduct business the same way they did in the past decade are not likely to be in business in the next decade. Antiquated business models might not fit newer business environments. Businesspeople need to be able to change with a market that is itself changing at a rapid rate.

Systemic effects

Inability to change not only affects the individual. It also profoundly impacts those around the individual. We are social creatures. Our ancestors lived in tribes. We hunted together; gathered food together; parented children together. We profoundly affect those we relate to in both overt and subconscious ways. I can't tell you how many times I've heard from executives how one supervisor's immature attitude can influence the entire team and work culture. People who do not change have a negative pull on those around them. This applies to families, friendships, churches and corporations.

The Yellow Brick Road

There are two ways to make change an intrinsic or a natural part of your life. One way is through repetition. If you repeat a behavior long enough, it becomes "second nature." Behavioral therapists believe that if you do something often enough over a given period of time, it will become habit. This can be good for physical habits such as a tennis stroke. But repetition is not always enough for emotional or psychological competencies, since personal and interpersonal habits are so complex and neurologically ingrained. For this kind of change, there is a second road: The Yellow Brick Road.

Along Dorothy's Yellow Brick Road, we find at least five practices,[5] any combination of which will bring about true learning and growth.

---

5. In previous editions of this book I used the term "discipline" because it contains the idea of learning, persistence and hard work. Webster defines discipline as: "the training that corrects, molds or perfects the mental facilities and moral character." When you hear the term discipline you are not likely to think of something easy, instant or quick. I replace "discipline" with practice

The term 'practice' includes the idea of acting in accordance with beliefs and values. It has the notion of repeating something in order to improve or establish healthy habits. The five practices of people who grow when life throws a tornado at them are:

- **Stay in the Land of Oz**
  We do not change in Kansas; we only change in the Land of Oz. Although uncharted and often difficult, the Land of Oz is the opportunity for growth and positive change. One needs to resist the temptation to leave the Land of Oz too soon and miss the many opportunities presented by staying the course.

- **Give up your Wizards**
  We must realize that our Wizards – the childish ideas about life, our self and others – are frauds. We have to release our Wizards in order to grow.

- **Integrate the Three Companions:**
  Scarecrow, Tin Man and Lion. It is when we, like Dorothy, bring together the positive manifestation of Tin Man heart, Lion courage and Scarecrow knowing, that we truly find inner harmony and become interpersonally effective.[6]

- **Face and melt your Witches**
  When we run from our witches they get bigger; it is only when we face our Witches that they melt. Every "hero" must eventually face something that is truly frightening in order to complete his or her journey.

---

because people gave me feedback that they could not identify with the term discipline. (Perhaps a sign of our times.) The term 'practice' is to round out the idea.

6. This third discipline, regarding Scarecrow Tin Man and Lion, is the foundation of this book.

- **Use your Resources**
  We must use all the resources at our disposal: Toto (our best friends and partners), Munchkins (the community), Glinda (our mentors) and the Ruby Slippers (our spirituality).

I've diagrammed these five practices below:[7]

In the following chapters, let's take a look together at each of these five practices from the *Yellow Brick Road* and see how they all ultimately lead to real change. These practices are especially important when a life-challenging twister throws us off balance. So if you are going through a difficult time in your life, I encourage you to see it as an opportunity to make vital course corrections that will improve and enrich your life. I

---

7. The disciplines are arranged this way to depict how all the disciplines are related to each other and interact with each other. It also shows that the third discipline regarding the three companions – Scarecrow, Tin Man and Lion—is the centerpiece of the disciplines. The other four disciplines organize around this discipline.

invite you to join Dorothy and her friends as they embark on the hero's journey and, if you dare, with them *follow the yellow brick road.*

REFLECTIONS

1. Make a list of the fictional and real-life heroes that capture your attention. Did they have to face and overcome any formidable challenges? If so what were they and how did they do it?

2. List times in your life when you had to face a significant challenge. How did you handle these times? Would you do anything different this time?

3. Can you identify any significant challenges that you are facing now (or anticipate facing)? Please list them and keep them in mind as you continue to read.

2. Stay in the LAND OF OZ

"Then you must go to the City of Emeralds ..."

"Where is this city?" asked Dorothy.

"It is exactly in the center of [the Land of Oz] ..."

"... How can I get there?" asked Dorothy.

"You must walk. It is a long journey, through a country that is sometimes pleasant and sometimes dark and terrible ... The road to the City of Emeralds is paved with yellow brick," said the [good] witch.

L. Frank Baum, *The Wonderful Wizard of Oz*

The Land of Oz is the strange country in which Dorothy lands after a twister carries off her house from Kansas. The Yellow Brick Road runs through the very center of the Land of Oz. If Dorothy had fled from the Land of Oz as soon as she arrived, she would never have met such interesting characters, undergone such exhilarating escapades, nor had the opportunity to grow from the entire experience. Her adventure would have been just a narrow escape rather than a life-changing odyssey.

The Land of Oz vs. Kansas

The best way to understand the Land of Oz is to compare it to Kansas.[8] Kansas represents everything that is established, secure and unchanging. Kansas is what we are used to. It is flat, has no bumps, no ridges, no mountains and no surprises; it is familiar and predictable. Our habits and our automatic thoughts and behaviors are Kansas. Kansas is home. Dorothy knows Kansas. She knows the rules of living in Kansas. She knows who the "good guys" are and who the "bad guys" are. However, when we find her there in the movie, she is bored and feels stuck, dreaming of somewhere over the rainbow.

The Land of Oz, on the other hand, is anything but boring. The Land of Oz is strange, unsettled and unfamiliar. The rules of Kansas don't work in the Land of Oz. When Dorothy arrives in the Land of Oz, she knows immediately that she is "not in Kansas anymore!" Oz is, by definition, lacking in definition. It is the vast unknown. When you are in the Land of Oz you are a foreigner in a foreign land with odd customs and strange faces. It is a place where anything can happen. Scarecrows talk, horses change color and monkeys fly! Dorothy is overwhelmed and disoriented when she finds herself in the Land of Oz, and her first impulse is to get back to Kansas as quickly as possible. She yearns for the predictability and stability of home.

The Land of Oz is not always bad but it is always uncharted. Whenever I travel, especially in a different culture, I am in "Oz." The customs are different and the streets are unknown. Often the inhabitants speak another language. I make many mistakes that I would not normally make when I am at home where I know the landscape. I make many fewer wrong turns on streets that are familiar to me. There is a cab driver in Italy, a merchant in Old Jerusalem and a camel driver in Egypt who have more of my hard-earned money than they should because I was in uncharted territory. The same is true when we learn new skills, such as a tennis stroke, a computer program or how to parent a child

---

8. I want to apologize to all readers who live (or have lived) in the state of Kansas. If L. Frank Baum picked another state to be in his story, I would have used *that* state as a metaphor.

for the first time (and a teenager at any time). At some time we are all "beginners" at something, and especially when we are we are in the Land of Oz.

Oz involves a great deal of "not knowing." When things get uncomfortable for clients during a session, they will automatically ask "why?" This is often an attempt to get back to Kansas, a place where things are *known*. There is nothing wrong with understanding and insight, but we usually want to bypass the uncomfortable process of discovery, the journey through the Land of Oz.

> *I have found that the best way to arrive at true "knowing" starts with being able to withstand a period of "not knowing."*

This is perhaps one of the most valuable lessons that I've learned as a therapist. I can remember as a new therapist feeling "Oz" crushing in on me when I conducted a session. The client would say something apparently important and I would not know what to say. Fearing the unknown, I would just start talking to fill in the silence. I have since come to find that when I can tolerate not knowing long enough, something usually occurs to me that is almost always more accurate, more creative and more pertinent than when I rush to fill in the "gap" of the unknown

The Land of Oz is full of gaps, empty spots of time and space that beg to be filled. Whether it was arriving in the strange land of the Munchkins, figuring out the idea of a "good" witch, or discovering apple trees that throw their apples at you, Dorothy found herself in situations where she was in need of being *filled in*.

People generally hate gaps, beginning with infancy. When an infant realizes that she is alone, she will often let out a blood-curdling scream as if to say, "somebody get over here right now and fill this gap!" Those of us who had a good experience with a mother who held us, soothed us and nurtured us in kind and loving ways have an advantage in life. But we all have to be weaned at some time. Then there is the gap. *The gap is Oz.*

The Land of Oz is never comfortable, but neither is it necessarily bad. The Land of Oz is where we grow and change. The Land of Oz represents the middle or transition phase of the hero's journey. The middle transition phase of the hero's journey occurs after the hero leaves the known life behind and before she returns a transformed person. The unknown filled with challenges and temptations characterizes this middle phase of the journey.

Change involves a combination of unlearning, disengagement and relearning, in close succession. I liken it to the changing of gears in an automobile with a standard transmission. You have to shift out of one gear and then into the next. In this analogy, the Land of Oz is the clutch. As we prepare to make a "paradigm shift,"[9] we engage that Oz clutch. This puts us in a psychological state of mind in which it becomes easier to suspend old paradigms and introduce better ones.

I have found this to be the case especially for those times when one's psychological house gets picked up by one of life's big twisters. People who are going through a break-up in a relationship, or just lost a loved one, or are struggling in business, or are going through a "midlife crisis" are often in the best position to make significant paradigm shifts.

One of the best literary examples of this comes from Charles Dickens' *The Christmas Carol*. It tells of a man who went through one remarkable Oz experience. Ebenezer Scrooge, a man who set a standard for greed and parsimony, was visited one Christmas Eve by the ghosts of Christmas Past, Present and Future. After this incredible, if not terrifying, Oz experience, he awakened a new man. He had an obvious paradigm shift.

People don't really change in this overnight, fairy-tale fashion. Rather, we go through a number of Oz experiences, which slowly create paradigm shifts. It is important to realize that we are not meant to stay

---

9. Stephen Covey, in his book *The Seven Habits of Highly Effective People*, describes paradigms as our internal "maps," or models, of ourselves and the world in which we live. These paradigms are the established ways in which we see ourselves, others and the world. A "paradigm shift" is an alteration or modification in these mental or emotional maps.

in Oz. We don't pack up and move there. The Land of Oz is a place of transition.

Kansas is not a bad place either. As a matter of fact, it is where we live most of the time. It's just hard to make changes while we are in Kansas. Actually, effective living involves alternating between Kansas and the Land of Oz. As we effectively move back and forth between these two places, each location changes the experience of living in the other. Every productive visit to the Land of Oz creates a more functional Kansas. The more effective and healthy our life in Kansas, the less difficult it is to revisit the Land of Oz. As we continue with this cycle, we develop a good life rhythm. So much so that we will be able to face the most difficult of life's experiences – even death.

After one of my speaking engagements, a man came up to me and jokingly asked if he could live in another state than Kansas. So I offered him California, known for its earthquakes. Then I got thinking about the analogy of earthquakes to the Oz experience.

Not all Oz experiences have the same intensity and duration. As there is a Richter scale for earthquakes, there is an Ozter Scale for psychological tremors. Earthquakes are measured for intensity and duration; so are Oz experiences. After an earthquake, a sense of fear/excitement takes hold, as Californians listen to radio and television reports to find out where the earthquake struck, how powerful it was and how long it lasted. It is interesting to note, however, that numerous earthquakes, not humanly discernible, hit California every week. Likewise, we have numerous *small* Oz experiences every day, but we don't always recognize them, even though they impact us. For example, you get stuck in a traffic jam; an employee is late with a report; you have a disagreement with your spouse; or you feel lonely or anxious. There can be *moderate* Oz experiences such as working with a difficult boss; going off to school; dating again after a divorce; starting a new job; or starting therapy.[10] And at some time, in every life, a big Oz-quake hits in the form

---

10. Oz experiences do not have to be negative. They just have to be different, unknown and uncomfortable.

of a serious illness, death of a loved one, winning the lottery (don't you wish?), losing a job or going through a divorce.[11]

Off-Ramps on the Yellow Brick Road

What does one have to do to get to the Land of Oz? Nothing! *Oz happens!* If you are alive and relatively conscious, you will repeatedly find yourself in the Land of Oz.

The real question is not getting to the Land of Oz; it's enduring your stay there. How does one stay in the Land of Oz long enough to harvest the benefits of being there?

Once I was standing in line with a child waiting to go on a roller-coaster ride. It was apparent that the ride was just too scary for him. The amusement park provided a last-chance escape in the line for people with cold feet to exit before the final turnstile, and we availed ourselves of it.

We all have built-in escape exits for ourselves when we end up in the Land of Oz. They're like off-ramps along the Yellow Brick Road offering us an early exit. I've noted four categories of off-ramp strategies:

Physical instead of soul

This first off-ramp is based on what Freud called the "pleasure principle." The pleasure principle is simple: Do things that make you *immediately* feel good and avoid anything that makes you feel bad. In the pleasure principle, the things that make you feel good usually involve physical sensations. Eating a high-calorie or high-fat treat, experiencing a sexual sensation, getting a rush of excitement from risky behavior or taking a mood-altering substance are all examples of this first off-ramp.

---

11. It would be a more significant moderate to severe Oz-quake that would qualify for the hero's journey (although a smaller event could still provoke a weakness to own and a challenge to face).

This off-ramp is very common among people who have compulsive personalities or are addiction-prone. People can be addicted to any number of substances or behaviors. I often see clients who compulsively use sex, food, alcohol, drugs, cigarettes and gambling. Sometimes they use these substances or behaviors simply out of habit. However, often these things are used to escape the Land of Oz. For example, let's say Pastor Jim (from Chapter One) gets in a fight with his wife or has trouble with the staff at church. He can stay on the Yellow Brick Road and endure the experience: feel sad, scared or mad and be proactive with his feelings. Or, he can "off-ramp" from the situation by visiting an adult bookstore instead. In the latter case, an Oz experience is avoided.

When people use physical methods to exit an Oz experience, they shortchange their soul. Soul comes from the Greek work *psyche*, which is the root word for psychology. *Psyche* translated means "life." The *psyche* is the seat of the feelings, desires and affections. For the ancient Greeks, the soul was an essence that differed from the body and could not be dissolved by death. Today we understand "soul" to be the emotional, moral and spiritual center of the human experience.

Whatever it means to you, the act of enduring Oz experiences matures the soul, whereas prolonged and constant avoidance of Oz stifles it. I do not have anything against sensuality for sensuality's sake; it is an essential part of the human experience. In fact, it can combine with the soul to give vitality to human experiences. The problem comes when the physical is used to escape Oz and nullify the soul.

Head instead of heart

I do not have anything against understanding, insight and knowledge either. In and of themselves they are beneficial. However, they do not serve well as a substitute for emotion or feelings. Feelings have their own benefit in the human experience. They provide outlets or tension reduction. Feelings can help motivate us. Feelings can actually stimulate thinking. Feelings also help us differentiate ourselves from others. However, most human beings seem to be afraid of pure emotion. Many people prefer to intellectualize rather than to feel. They would rather know why they are having an experience than experiencing the experience. *Going into your head* is the second escape mechanism or off-ramp. When an Oz experience is in process, we often escape by over-thinking, by intellectualizing or obsessing.

Obsession occurs when the mind is completely overtaken by one idea. It comes from the Latin word *obsessus* that means 'besieged.' People who are besieged by an idea are usually stuck in their capacity to feel freely (except when they feel badly about what they are obsessing about). This is a painful psychological phenomenon for the person and those around him.

I know someone who abused alcohol for several years. He eventually "hit bottom" and subsequently took control over his life. He got into a twelve-step program, involved himself in personal therapy, stopped using alcohol and turned his life around. Unfortunately, his wife was never able to accept his rehabilitation. She continued to worry about her husband resuming his alcoholism and agonized over it every day, in spite of the positive evidence to the contrary. Her obsessing was excruciating for everyone in the family. When she finally stopped obsessing years later, she was hit by a myriad of deep and painful feelings, stemming from her own personal life. As it turns out, the obsessing about her husband's drinking was her way to avoid the issues of her own life – an exit off *her* Yellow Brick Road. The onset of these deep feelings represented her arrival in the Land of Oz.

Mania instead of sadness

Sadness is part of living and a vital part of the Land of Oz. It is the normal response to loss and limits. *If you are fully human, you cannot not feel sad.* Life is full of losses and limits. Mania is a defense against being sad. Mania, according to Webster's, is "extravagant enthusiasm." An individual in the throes of mania feels they are able to triumph over life's limits and losses. Often mania is mistaken for confidence or a positive mental outlook. Mania is about *not* feeling sad more than about being positive or confident. Mania can be very destructive.[12]

Often, when clients get close to a meaningful – I would call it Oz – connection, their voices and thoughts speed up. They become manic. I will sometimes ask them how fast they would be going if they were in a car. They almost always look at me with an embarrassed smile and say they would be going over the legal speed limit. If they were not speeding, they might have "slowed" down enough to end up in the Land of Oz.

Another version of mania is what I call "occupating." Occupating is a combination of mania and obsessing, when one is continually trying to keep every moment filled. It is funny how often I hear versions of the following story: A person being visited by out-of-town parents reports that one of the parents – typically the father – occupates from the time that they arrive until they leave a few days later. The parent will assess the premises of the house and then start a never-ending crusade to clean, fix, build and rebuild things. Except for meals and sleep, they would keep on going if no one stopped them. They are occupating: filling every minute with activity. With occupating, you end up with a very clean house and a parent who has escaped the Land of Oz. When we constantly fill every minute with words, work, hobbies, Internet, television – any kind of activity for that matter – we are avoiding the experience-in-the-moment that I refer to as the Land of Oz. We also avoid the opportunity to grow.

Anger can be another form of mania. Some people who are trying to escape an Oz experience become irritable and angry. They want to blame others and become critical of those around them. They are edgy. Being in Oz is vulnerable; being sad is vulnerable.

Anger can be a "quick fix" to not feel vulnerable and sad.

---

12. When I use the term mania here, I am not equating it to the very serious disorder of manic-depression, which is an extreme form of mania and generally has biochemical aspects to it. Manic-depression is generally treated with medication and psychotherapy.

We see this happening with the Lion when we first meet him. If you remember, Dorothy, Scarecrow, Tin Man and Toto entered a scary forest. There they were accosted by a lion that snarled and roared at them in order to intimidate them. Dorothy subsequently confronted him for threatening her dog. It is then that we find out that the lion is nothing more than a coward. Lion was insecure because he was not doing well at being King, so he maniacally took it out on the weaker members of Dorothy's delegation.

Depression instead of sadness

This fourth way to avoid Oz is tricky. ***Some people avoid Oz by beating Oz to the punch.*** In other words, they stay miserable most of the time. They feel they have a franchise on a troubled life. In the book version, *The Wonderful Wizard of Oz*, Aunt Em is depicted as very negative and depressed, living in an unmercifully flat and gray Kansas farmland. "She was thin and gaunt and never smiled."

For people in a "depressed" Kansas,[13] what is "stable" is their instability. They live out a life script that says something like this: "My early life was difficult, and now it is all that I know. I am used to things not working out for me and I am resigned to things going badly. In fact, I even get benefits from it: People sometimes feel sorry for me. I don't have to expect much for myself and, most of all, I am never surprised by the twists and turns of life."

> *Sadness is the emotional response to living life without painkillers.*

It is what some philosophers call "authentic suffering." The experience of authentic suffering includes our aloneness in the world, the limits of time and resources, and the pain of lost love. Sadness is an experience

---

13. When I use the term depressed here, I am not referring to the biologically based depression that is often treated with medication.

of the Land of Oz. Some people have found a way to use "inauthentic" suffering to avoid the authentic suffering of the Land of Oz.

This may raise questions from some people. How can a person live in misery to avoid sadness? I have sat with many people who are absolutely conversant with self-hate but will avoid *not-knowing* and sadness like the plague. Some will stay miserable at work (and make others miserable as well) rather than risk being kind. Others will stay in highly abusive relationships rather than live life on their own.[14]

How to Benefit From a Visit to the Land of Oz

But Dorothy stays on the Yellow Brick Road and endures the Land of Oz. You might argue that she did not have a choice. She was transported there by a twister and had no way to escape. You could continue to argue that she did everything she could to get out of Oz and back to Kansas. I would agree. Our primal inclination is to get back home, to the place of familiarity.[15] However, what is important is that Dorothy does in fact stay on the Yellow Brick Road in the Land of Oz. And while there, she does face weakness (underdeveloped Scarecrow, Tin Man and Lion) and challenges (melting witches and defrocking wizards) long enough to grow and change.

In real life, people can get out of Oz much easier than Dorothy could. I've already mentioned at least four general ways in which this happens. Even when the twister of life picks them up and drops them in a place that seems to have no escape, some people still leave the Land of Oz too soon.

I remember being told a story about a man whose wife died. This man lived what appeared to be a successful life. He coped with life stresses in

14. However, it is a wonder to watch these "depressed" people learn to endure the Land of Oz. As they start to let go of the Kansas misery that they have known all their lives, they open themselves to a whole new world full of color and aliveness.

15. Unless, of course, we are in an *alpha* mode, which is naturally oriented toward growth and change. (See Chapter One).

seemingly strong ways. In truth, however, he was remarkably efficient at exiting Oz. The day after his wife died, he collected all her things, called the local thrift store and had them come and pick them up. He hardly ever talked about her after that and never showed any evidence of grieving. Unlike Dorothy, he did not benefit from being in the Land of Oz. He did not benefit from grieving the loss of his partner. He escaped.

It's what we don't do

As it pertains to this practice, it is not what we do that is important. It is what we don't do. If we *don't* do the behaviors that help us escape the Land of Oz, we can stay there long enough to learn, grow and change. If we don't jump back into the old style of thinking and coping, we will continue on the hero's journey until the end. This may sound simple. It is simple yet profoundly difficult.

In the book version, *The Wonderful Wizard of Oz*, Dorothy was often challenged to stay on the Yellow Brick Road. Sometimes by choice, more often due to obstacles, she and her three companions would become sidetracked. Together they shared many escapades getting back onto the Yellow Brick Road. It might be likened to trying to stay on the soccer field of life instead of running off the field and out of bounds. It's just that the lines are not always as clear and obvious as on a soccer field. As a therapist and business consultant, I often see my role as one that indicates to a client when he or she is playing out of bounds.

The art of authentic suffering

We live in a society that has mastered the art of convenient and immediate gratification. Technology has made it possible for our needs and wishes to be met and our pain and suffering to be alleviated at faster and faster rates. We can obtain a meal – if you can call it a meal – from start to finish in just a few minutes, alleviate pain with drugs and have sex with a stranger over the telephone. We live in a society that promises, and sometimes provides, quick money, fast diets, extended youth and easy answers. Corporations sometimes only see as far as the next shareholders' meeting or quarterly profit report. We have lost the art of suffering.

The art of suffering is *not* masochism. Masochism is the act of deriving gratification from being physically or emotionally abused, or getting a secondary gain from being pained, offended, dominated or mistreated. In short, masochism is the tendency to seek pain. It is the turning of destructive tendencies upon oneself. It is the attraction toward unnecessary suffering. Authentic suffering is none of this.

Authentic suffering has to do with the capacity to endure an uncomfortable or painful experience over the time it needs to be experienced – no more and no less – in order to maintain one's honesty and integrity and to avoid the damage that results from evading the experience. It is the ability to stay in the Land of Oz for as long as you need to stay. Children do not know how to do this. They need a parent's help over time to learn how to endure the real, unavoidable, part-of-living pain until, as adults, they can do this on their own. "Endurance" means continuing in the same condition; it means remaining firm while in suffering or discomfort without yielding. It has to do with experiencing an Oz state without avoiding or escaping.

Let me offer two illustrations of endurance.

In my practice I regularly deal with sex addiction. A man walks down the street, sees a very attractive woman and is stirred sexually. The difference between a sex addict and a person who is not addicted is that the non-compulsive person will experience, endure and maybe even enjoy the sexual experience until it runs its normal course. The sex addict, on the other hand, is so stirred by the stimulation that he will immediately start to obsess about and plan his next sexual "binge." This dilemma specific to sex addiction actually applies to any situation in life where we cannot endure an experience long enough without having a harmful reaction to it.

After losing a loved one we enter a natural period of intense grieving. We are expected to feel depressed and angry. This is non-masochistic suffering, and, if we endure, we get to the other side of the grieving process. As a result, we are able to move on with our lives, having integrated the person we lost into our hearts and minds. Most often we grow from the experience.

Acknowledge and endure

We are taught at a young age to delay gratification. We are told that we can't have any dessert until we've eaten dinner. Children have to wait for their birthdays or for holidays. We teach them to "hold" their temper until they calm down. After dinner comes dessert; after a week is Halloween; after the temper is held, one feels better. After Oz, comes a better Kansas. We need to know deep inside that Oz ends. *Oz does not go on forever.*

We need to acknowledge six things:

1.   **Oz happens.** Instability and discomfort are just as much part of life as stability and comfort. We get both. Normal living alternates between Oz and Kansas every day, as it does throughout life. Life is neither fair nor unfair. Many people would like to believe that if they do everything just so, the Land of Oz can and should be avoided. This is not true.

     Oz happens! Life is difficult; we need to accept it. Then we will be free.

2.   **No one can avoid Oz without a cost.** Here are the choices: We can endure the Land of Oz now without any interest or penalties, or we can pay later with high interest, debt and obligations. If we use television, drugs, blame, victim playing, materialism, work, sex, rationalization to avoid Oz NOW, we end up with a psychological, physical and spiritual debt LATER. We have the choice. I know that it is not easy when we are going through an especially painful time in our life. Sometimes we need a break

for a while. However, taking a conscious break is not the same as using denial or destructive behaviors to escape.

3. **The stay in Oz is temporary.** Dorothy did not know that her visit to Oz would end. A person in grief worries that her sadness will never end. This is a leftover from our childhood. Young children are not aware of time in the same way as adults and therefore do not realize that emotional states are temporary. For example, when a young child sees his mother leave he worries that she will never come back. When a child feels hungry or angry or sad, it is as if that is ALL that he will feel FOREVER. If they are fortunate enough to have a parent that can adequately soothe their fears and reassure them, they learn to endure. They will learn that the stay in the Land of Oz does not last forever.

4. **After Oz comes true peace.** The paradox is that people who can tolerate Oz are also the most peaceful people. People who chronically avoid Oz are often in a state of agitation, resentment, worry and discomfort.

5. **Oz builds strength and character.** People who master this practice are the most able to live in life as it is. They have true confidence that comes from inner security. Dorothy grew to be a stronger and more confident woman after going through her Oz experience. She will be more realistic in her expectations and more appreciative in everyday living.

6. **Oz is a wonderful place to visit.** The cyclone had set the house down, very gently – for a cyclone – in the midst of a country of marvelous beauty. There were lovely patches of green sward all about, with stately trees bearing rich and luscious fruits. Banks of gorgeous flowers were on every hand and birds with rare and

brilliant plumage sang ... very grateful to a little girl who had lived so long on the dry gray prairies.[16]

The Land of Oz is a land full of color. When we can endure the difficult or painful parts of the Land of Oz, we are then able to enjoy the wonderful aspects of Oz! Actually, many of Dorothy's experiences in the Land of Oz are awe-inspiring and wonderful. The Land of Oz can be a place of creativity, invention and spirituality. People who can stay on this *road less traveled* can often think of a solution that no one else does in the work team. While in Oz we naturally say the right thing at the right time to our boss, spouse, child or client.

While in Oz we write the lyric, we paint the work of art, love the beloved and sing with passion. In the Land of Oz we find our Self, the Cherished and God.

For those of us who can endure, the Land of Oz is a truly wonderful place.

---

16. L. Frank Baum, *The Wonderful Wizard of Oz*

REFLECTIONS

1.   What life-tornadoes have picked up you house in your lifetime? How would you rate their intensity? Have any tornadoes picked up your house recently?

2.   When confronted with a Land of Oz experience, what off-ramps are you more likely to take? How (be specific)?

3.   What would happen if you did not leave, but instead stayed on the Yellow Brick Road? What are you afraid of or concerned about?

4.   What benefits have you experienced by staying the course on the Yellow Brick Road?

3. Give up your WIZARDS

The Tin Woodman ... rushed toward the little man and cried out, "Who are you?"

"I am Oz, the Great and Terrible," said the little man, in a trembling voice, "but don't strike me – please don't ..."

L. Frank Baum, *The Wonderful Wizard of Oz*

It is quite possible that there is not a more deadly state of mind than idealism. Whether it is destructive to one individual's self esteem, or to an entire company's morale, idealization is harmful.

Yet Dorothy and her three companions are on a quest for an ideal. They are searching for the great and wonderful Wizard of Oz. The Wizard is one who is going to make everything all better! *If only* they can get to him, *then* Scarecrow would have a brain, Tin Man a heart, Lion courage and Dorothy would find her way back home to Kansas.

Many of us are on a similar quest. We believe that *if only* we could find our wizards, *then* we would find happiness and a sense of importance, safety and security. Then perhaps we would escape life's difficulties and not have to battle with the struggles that naturally go along with being human

Remember what happens to Dorothy and her three companions after they do all that the Wizard of Oz has requested of them – including bringing back the broomstick from the Wicked Witch? Having pushed all limits to meet his requisites, they come before him to collect their promised rewards. However, the Wizard is not so quick to fulfill their wishes. In fact, he is quick to require even more of them, as do most of our personal wizards. But then something very important happens. As only a good friend would do, Dorothy's dog, Toto, exposes the truth: He pulls back the curtain that hides the so-called Wizard from view and exposes him as a *fraud*. The Wizard cannot deliver what he promised. He cannot award a brain, a heart, courage, a home ... or, through any of these things, happiness. He cannot help them after all.

When we are thrown into the unknown Land of Oz by one of life's many tornados, we often look for someone or something to deliver us.

This is not to be confused with wanting an outside resource to help us, which is a well-founded need. Instead it seems that we put all our energies into being rescued by some magical power outside ourselves rather than facing and resolving the situation at hand.

The goal of this chapter is to pull back the curtain from our personal wizards. It is to reveal that no matter what we do to serve them, they will never be able to give us happiness, inner peace or relief from natural human limits and struggle. Wizards will NOT help us to recover and grow from the disturbing tornados that inevitably come our way, and they certainly will not help us find our way home. To find what we seek in our lives, we must take responsibility for it ourselves. This usually takes hard work. There are no shortcuts if you actually want to grow. Everyone must journey down his or her own personal Yellow Brick Road.

Idealism: A Definition

In order to appreciate what idealism is, let's first look at what idealism is *not*.

- **Idealism is not ideals.** Ideals, values, ethics and good taste are important. By ideals, I mean standards of maturity, beauty or excellence. Ideals are goals we aim for and models we follow. Ideals give life substance and meaning. Idealism is not ideals.

- **Idealism is not desire or ambition.** Idealism might generate desire or ambition, but it is not the same. We cannot develop or better ourselves without ambition, goal setting or desire. We *can* improve ourselves without idealism.

- **Idealism is not hope**. Hope is one of the more healthful mental attitudes. Hope is necessary for a successful and enjoyable life and is essential for anyone going through a life challenge. A person who is idealistic is not a person who is hopeful. In fact, idealism inevitably fosters despair. Because idealism is not based in reality it will eventually lead to disappointment and discouragement, the opposite of hope.

- **Idealism is not a positive mental attitude.** A person who has a true and intrinsic *positive mental attitude* will more than likely not have many wizards dictating his or her actions. Some individuals exude a positive mental attitude that is merely a disguise for idealism. They grab onto empty slogans, or have attitudes that don't take into account the realities of life. It is easy to talk about it, but quite another thing to actually posses a truly positive mental attitude.

Idealism is the belief in and pursuit of perfection *as if* it were an attainable goal. Please note, it is both the fanciful idea and its pursuit. First the belief is unrealistic. In fact idealism is the opposite of realism. Second, that which is idealized becomes the aim of any endeavor. In this respect, idealism drives us.[17]

---

17. For those of you who care, idealism is also a philosophical theory that states ultimate reality lies in a realm transcending phenomena; that material things do not exist independently but only as constructions in the mind.

For nearly three decades I have observed wizards[18] operating within my clients – both clinical and with organizations. Likewise, I have experienced the dominion of wizard-wanting within myself. In this respect, I have found that wizards have at least three interrelated components: imagination, tantalization and satisfaction. Let's take a closer look at each of these, beginning first with *imagination*.

When we "fall in love" with someone, we generally do not really know the person to whom we are attracted. Early on in a romantic relationship, the object of our affection is likely to be essentially an image in our head or fantasy rather than being seen from a realistic appraisal. We fill in the blanks and the gaps with all the lovely and exciting things we want in a partner.[19] This example illustrates the fact that wizards exist primarily in our imagination.

One of the definitions of idealism is that of "viewing life through rose-tinted glasses." It is interesting to note that in the book, Dorothy and her companions (including Toto) were all required to wear emerald-tinted glasses *at all times* while in the Emerald City! Therefore, it made even ordinary stone look like precious metal. When we are in the throes of wanting a wizard, we in essence are wearing the very same emerald-tinted glasses.

"… Dorothy dreamed of the Emerald City, and of the good Wizard Oz, who would soon send her back to her own home again."[20]

Our wizards do not exist out there in reality. They live only in the Emerald City of our mind. They exist in the magical place in our mind where we dream, in our imagination.

---

18. From now on and whenever I can I will use the term *Wizard* to represent idealism.

19. Later on, if the relationship fizzles, we may turn around and project all the things we fear and hate onto that same person.

20. Baum, *op. cit.*

The second aspect of wizards involves what is called *tantalization*. W. R. D. Fairbairn was a prominent psychoanalyst working in the beginning of the Twentieth Century. He described an important psychological dynamic. He stated that to the degree a child's basic emotional needs were consistently frustrated, the child develops two mental states, one of which he referred to as tantalizing.[21] In this tantalizing state of mind, the person – even as an adult – becomes maniacally *excited* and absorbed by unrealistic, if not magical, ideas about himself, another person or an aspect of life. These enticements can be very potent and can blind the person to all other information and considerations.

I work with some people who become preoccupied, even obsessed, with another person – often in a romantic way. When they encounter or even think about this person, they become very keyed up and excited. If the relationship is dysfunctional, as they often are, it is very difficult for the person to leave the relationship even if it is harmful. This is often what it is like with wizards.

> *Our wizards – those things we view through emerald-tinted glasses – tend to tickle and excite us beyond what is realistic and balanced.*

Third, wizards convey a notion of *promised satisfaction*. "You must keep your promises to us!" Dorothy exclaimed to the Wizard when she returns from melting the Wicked Witch. Wizards promise us what we don't think we can adequately provide for ourselves. This desire comes from within us. "How can I help being a humbug," the Wizard said, "when all these people make me do things that everybody knows can't be done?"

Wizards work on the "If only … then …" principle. *If only* I get the Wizard, *then* I will be given a brain, heart, courage or home. The "if only" is the wizard (for example, "If only I had more money, a great figure, a better spouse or loving children, a nicer car, or some other desir-

---

21. Fairbairn's second or "persecutory" mental state is very similar to that of the Witch. This "witch" state of mind will be covered in Chapter Five.

able thing"). The "then" part of the formula has to do with fulfilling the promise – the essential desire or satisfaction (for example, "then I would be happy or feel worthwhile").

When we have these three dynamics working together, imagination (vs. reality), tantalization and promised satisfaction, wizards truly become a very powerful and destructive force in a person, family or organization.

In essence, the pursuit of wizards represents the wish to return to the Garden of Eden. In the Garden of Eden, God takes care of Adam and Eve. Everything they need is provided. They are safe and protected. They move about their "home" freely without fear or guilt. They sense that they belong and are loved. The "Big Parent" knows everything that is needed to know and can do everything that needs to be done.

This wish to return to the Garden is a wish to return to an "All-Good-Parent" or Wizard. It is a desire to have a Mommy or Daddy, who loves us unconditionally, keeps us safe and provides everything we need. Who wouldn't want to live in that type of situation? We all want to abide in a place where we are nurtured and cared for and nothing bad happens to us. This wish to return to the Garden is the engine that powers our pursuit of wizards. It was the same wish driving Dorothy to find the Great and Wonderful Wizard of Oz.

Different Types of Wizards

Wizards take on many forms. In the movie version of *The Wizard of Oz,* the Wizard appears as a large man's face immersed in smoke and fire. However, in the book, each character perceives him differently. To Dorothy, he is a large head; to the Scarecrow, a beautiful woman; to the Tin Man, a beast; and to the Lion, a fierce ball of fire.

Our personal wizards also appear to us in many forms. The following are just a few of the ways we romanticize people or situations and thus turn them into *wizards*.

Wizards as our idealized selves

Most people have an idealized view of themselves. Some people have a very exaggerated idealized view of themselves and consequently become arrogant and egotistical. We call these people narcissistic.[22] They use their emerald-tinted view of themselves as a protection against their insecurity and pain. It is not true confidence at all but instead an excited, tantalizing even omnipotent view of their selves. The problem is that narcissistic people continually have to keep up their romantic view of themselves; otherwise, they experience a great deal of negative emotions and a feeling of failure or very low self-worth.

Other people who are more shame based develop feelings of self-doubt and inadequacy because they are constantly falling short of the idealistic view of themselves. In fact, most people who have poor self-images also have idealized views of their own selves that are the standard against which they feel inferior. Part of maturity is the acquisition of a sober (non-tantalizing), realistic estimate of oneself. When we know and accept ourselves – strengths and weakness alike – we will have a healthier self-image. Otherwise, we are constantly chasing our "wizard selves," saying things like, "*If only* I were more this or I were less that or able to do this better, *then* I would be acceptable."

Idealized-others wizards

Because I live in California, I occasionally run into a celebrity, and I must confess that I find myself fascinated with them. Why? Sometimes it's because they are truly interesting people. Most of the time, however, it has more to do with the human tendency to idolize – thus idealize – people. Our *imagination* makes them bigger than life. We get excited when we see them: "If only" we were like them or we knew them, then *we* would be important.

---

22. Narcissus was a character in Greek mythology, a beautiful young boy who was carried away by the love of his own reflection. He was turned into a flower, which now bears his name.

We romanticize all sorts of people apart from celebrities. We idealize people we depend upon, such as bosses, clergy, physicians, psychotherapists. We idealize "experts." Understand that I am not talking about the respect we would naturally have for these people in their particular areas of expertise. Idealization involves imagining these people to be far greater – in every area of life – than they really are or even possibly could be.

Some people idealize anyone other than themselves. They have a particular style whereby they automatically attribute superior qualities to other people, whether or not that view is legitimate.[23] This is the case when someone meets a perfect stranger and automatically attributes superior qualities to that stranger before they ever get to know them.

Romantic love wizards

Romantic love entails falling in love with "falling in love." It is seldom founded on knowledge of or true respect for the other person. Rather, romantic love springs from a tantalizing psycho-chemical reaction based on our evolutionary urge to mate. Even the most logical person can be struck by Cupid's arrow. Romantic love is the originator of countless babies, thousands of songs, most marriages, many divorces, a few wars and plenty of heartaches. Like all wizards, it turns out to be less than it promised to be. For those of us who hang in there after the idealism wears off, who work to develop an enduring realistic relationship based on mutual acceptance and respect, a stable and loving partnership can replace the idealized love.

"The easy life" wizards

M. Scott Peck starts his classic book, *The Road Less Traveled,* with words that would only be necessary in an affluent society: "Life is dif-

---

23. We will cover the "moving – toward" personality style in the next chapter on the three companions.

ficult." Modern, affluent societies think that life should be easy. We should be able to have a "drive-through" existence where we can get what we want when we want it. People are often surprised when things go wrong, as if something abnormal has happened. They say that life is unfair. The truth is that life is neither fair nor unfair. Life is difficult; it always has been and always will be. Our idealization of life will not change this.

Physical appearance wizards

We are a society that worships beauty. There is everything to like about a beautiful woman or a handsome man, but when it becomes a wizard it cannot produce what is promised – true happiness and security. At best, this wizard distracts resources (time, money, energy, etc.) away from other more important concerns of living. People think, "if only I were taller, thinner, tighter, larger, and smaller … then I would be happy or loveable." They then pursue this wizard with a passion. At worst, it is the basis of self-loathing or prejudice and even anorexia and bulimia. The pressure on people, especially females in this regard, is enormous. Society and culture decide what is beautiful, and we in turn made it into a wizard.

In a similar way, we make youth a wizard.[24] There is nothing wrong with wanting to be healthy and in good shape. The obsession with being youthful goes way beyond a realistic interest in health. It is a wizard promising us that we will be happy or significant "if only" we are beautiful as only youth can be. If we age – even with good health and fitness – we are defective. To this wizard, a wrinkle is a scar.

Wizards as materialism and wealth

Why do we respond to someone who drives a Mercedes differently than to someone who drives a Honda? Why do we seldom question the

---

24. Unless you are young, then you idealize being older.

fact that the CEO of a large corporation receives up to 100 times more money than the principal of a grammar school? Why do we have bumper stickers that say, "The one who dies with the most toys wins?" Need I say more?

Dogma wizards

Whether it is a religious belief, a political party, a corporate philosophy or a psychological theory, we idealize dogma. Dogma is a word that comes from the Latin, *dogma*, meaning something that we hold as an established truth, often without adequate grounds. I am not talking here about deeply held personal beliefs. I am referring here to a rigid adherence to ideas that goes beyond the scope of the ideas. A good example of this comes from my own profession. Most people I know eventually establish an operating psychological theory. However, some people espouse a theory so much that they almost make a religious practice out of it. Their clients have to fit the theory rather than the other way around. What was once a theory has now become a road map to a Wizard. Such fanatical adherence to systems of belief – such as fascism, communism, extreme right wing or extreme left wing political movements and even religious movements – has cost literally millions of lives.

Off-ramp wizards

We idealize anything that helps us escape the chaotic *Land of Oz*. Any person or behavior that gets us out of uncomfortable or emotionally painful experiences is a candidate for becoming a wizard. If you are an alcoholic, alcohol is your wizard; if you are a sex addict, pornography, prostitutes, or a succession of lovers are your wizards; if you use work to escape emptiness in your life, work is your wizard. Each of these wizards serves the same purpose – to provide an off-ramp from our journey along the Yellow Brick Road.

If you want to know what we are idealizing these days, you merely have to look at advertisements on the web, television or in magazines. More often than not, they feature something that we idealize. You will see either a very attractive woman, a well-dressed man in an expensive car, two people lost in love or smiling people smoking cigarettes. Why do advertisers use idealism?

As long as we are looking for wizards, wizards sell.

The Advantages and Disadvantages of Idealism

I can think of only one benefit of idealism. Idealism is necessary for children. Young children are not ready for what *Genesis* calls the "knowledge of good and evil." They still need the Garden of Eden; they still need someone to take care of things for them. They need to feel unconditionally loved, nurtured and safe. Children require protection and temporary insulation from the real world. They need room to play and learn necessary skills. Gradually, over the course of development, a loved and protected child builds the capacity to live in the world as it is – without wizards.

The disadvantages of idealism are far more numerous. I will briefly mention a few of the liabilities.

Wizards foster and maintain immaturity

"Because you are strong and I am weak. Because you are a Great Wizard and I am only a helpless little girl." [25] The pursuit of Wizards requires us to act small and to stay young.

As we have already discussed, implicit in the pursuit of wizards is a wish to return to the Garden of Eden – the "Kansas" of our ideal childhood. Because this is a requirement of the young, people who pursue

---

25. Baum, op. cit.

wizards inevitably keep themselves young. To put it another way, when people put their energies in finding and keeping wizards, they do not grow and mature. Consider an extraordinarily attractive woman who, because of her looks, gets more than average attention, perks and job promotions. Unless she has good, intrinsic work values and integrity, it would be easy for her to rely on her external looks and never develop the inner person. Likewise, people with a good deal of money, especially if they did not have to work for it, often do not have to develop the inner skills and discipline that naturally mature us.

Wizards create a welfare state

To give something to adults on an ongoing basis without expecting anything in return does not help people grow – not to mention feel good about themselves. I personally believe welfare should be a stopgap measure, but when it becomes a way of life, it is psychologically damaging.[26] When it becomes a way of life the government becomes a wizard.

I often hear about able-bodied adults who are still dependent on their parents for income and shelter. Sometimes, one spouse is on emotional welfare with the other spouse. Scarecrow gets a brain by learning from experience and struggle, not because the Wizard gives him one. The same was true for Tin Man's heart and Lion's courage. People who depend on a wizard will not have the manifold benefits of doing things on their own.

Wizards foster hatred toward others

There is a rule in psychology which states that we end up hating those we depend on. This is certainly true in regard to those people we make into wizards. People who follow wizards end up angry and disappointed. Ralph, for example, sets his wife up as a wizard. He expects her to give him more than is realistically possible. Because of the "welfare state"

---

26. This does not include significantly handicapped or chronically ill people.

that he has with her and because of her inevitable failures to make him happy, he harbors a great deal of resentment. At times, these resentments come out as outbursts of rage and criticism. People who pursue wizards end up being angry with the people they pursue.

Wizards foster aversion to reality

> *"I have been making believe."*
>
> *"Making believe!" cried Dorothy. "Are you not a Great Wizard?"*
>
> *"Hush my dear," he said; "don't speak so loud, or you will be overheard – and I should be ruined. I'm supposed to be a Great Wizard."* ...
>
> *"Doesn't anyone else know you're a humbug?" asked Dorothy.*
>
> *"No one knows it but you four – and myself," replied Oz. "I have fooled everyone so long that I thought I should never be found out."*[27]

The truth be told, there is no Wizard! We no longer live in the Garden of Eden. As adults, we have to live on the third planet in our solar system – just as it is. On this planet, we do not have a visible All-present Big Parent-Wizard that makes things easy, safe and understandable. Even those of us who have a deep faith about a personal God cannot escape this reality.

Reality keeps reminding us that there is very little in life that is perfect. For this reason, we often reject reality instead of listening to it. We create our own alternate realities that better fit the wish for the Wizard. We prefer to fool ourselves even as the Wizard fooled everyone for so long. If someone tells us the truth, we fight what is said rather than

---

27. Baum, *op. cit.*

change our imagined reality.[28] As a result, we come to hate what is true and real, because it challenges our wishes.

Wizards generate envy

People who idealize tend to see the things they *wish* for all around them, which generates a tremendous amount of envy.[29] If you idealize having perfect children, you will constantly imagine that you see near-perfect kids everywhere you see children. If you idealize what a spouse can magically do for your happiness, you will envy other people's spouses.

There is always someone who is smarter, taller, shorter, richer, faster, thinner, to envy.

Instead of learning to be satisfied with who he is and what he can do, the idealist is constantly plagued with wizard-driven envy.

Wizards provide a very low return on your investment

People spend an inordinate amount of resources in pursuit of their wizards. The problem is that when they get what they have been striving for they still come up shortchanged. They exert more energy and expend more time than they ever get in return. People with perfect bodies still don't necessarily like themselves; people with a lot of money still don't get genuine respect; people with power are still out of control. And even though Dorothy apprehended the witch's broom, the Wizard still did not

---

28. For example: "You drink too much"; "You need to see a doctor about your lump"; "Your mother is too immature to ever love and accept you the way you would like"; "Your unhappiness is not because of your spouse;" "Your executive management team is in trouble."

29. I find envy – as a state of mind – to be one of the more powerful and destructive states of mind (not to mention emotionally very painful).

give Scarecrow knowing, Tin Man heart, Lion courage, nor Dorothy a way back home.

Some Important Things to Know About Wizards

There is some truth in the appeal of most wizards

I have heard it said that the best lie has some truth in it. People typically idealize someone or something that has positive attributes. It becomes a wizard, not because it is either good or bad, but because of what we wish the Wizard would do for us. In other words, it is not that money, an attractive mate or successful careers are in and of themselves bad. They become harmful when they excite us to the point of preoccupation. They become wizards when we think they hold the key to ultimate personal happiness.

The phenomenon of wizards is primarily "subconscious"

Most people would not be able to identify the person or things that they make into wizards, for it usually has little to do with the rational, conscious side of the mind. Most educated people, when asked to discuss idealism, would probably agree that little or nothing is ideal. What is important is not what we believe but how we behave. When a person is on a crusade for the wizard, everything they subconsciously believe propels them to act as if something is going to bring them back to the Garden. Another word for 'subconscious' is 'automatic.' And often we *automatically* start pursuing wizards without ever thinking.

Relinquishing wizards is a difficult process

Often in the hero's journey the most difficult challenge comes last. Could this be true for Dorothy? One would think that facing the witch was Dorothy's most difficult task. But in the story it was only after she melted the witch that she was able to face the realization that her Wonderful Wizard was neither wonderful nor a wizard, he was a fraud. I have worked with many clients who had to face some scary part of themselves before they could give up some unrealistic view of themselves or their life.

Wizards ask more of us than they give

I'll let the Wizard tell you about this one himself. He told Dorothy when asking what she wanted from him that "You have no right to expect me to send you back to Kansas unless you do something for me in return. In this country everyone must pay for everything he gets. If you wish me to use my magic power to send you home again you must do something for me first." [30]

Application: How We Can Grow

We are never more prone to pursue a wizard as when we are in the Land of Oz. Just ask Dorothy. It is when we are upset, discouraged, resentful, grieving or lonely that we automatically start to look for our personal wizards. It is at these times, more than ever, we need to change course and follow three simple but not-so-easy steps. We will look briefly at each of these steps.

Realize that your wizard is a fraud

Toto jumped away ... and tipped over the screen that stood in a corner. As it fell with a crash they looked that way, and the next moment all of them were filled with wonder. For they saw, standing in just the spot the screen had hidden, a little old man,

---

30. Baum, *op. cit.*

with a bald head and a wrinkled face, who seemed to be as much surprised as they were. The Tin Woodman, raising his axe, rushed towards the little man and cried out, "Who are you?"

"I am Oz, the Great and Terrible," said the little man, in a trembling voice, "but don't strike me." [31]

Most people don't give up their wizards easily. Most of us in Dorothy's position would have ignored the old man over in the corner and continued to try to win the approval and deliverance of the Great and Wonderful Oz. If we are going to grow when life throws us into the Land of Oz, we first have to be impacted by the realization that the wizard is a **fraud**.

Work through the grieving process

And that was the last any of them ever saw of Oz, the Wonderful Wizard ... But the people remembered him lovingly, and said to one another, "Oz was always our friend. When he was here he built for us this beautiful Emerald City." Still, for many days they grieved over the loss of the Wonderful Wizard, and would not be comforted. [32]

The natural emotional and psychological response to this realization is grief. After we truly come to terms with the wizard being a fraud, we are faced with a loss. And the "normal" response to loss is grief. According to Elizabeth Kubler-Ross, the first reaction in grieving is typically to minimize, or even deny, the loss. However, if the person is en route to working through the loss, he soon will alternate between anger and sadness.[33] After he goes through this roller-coaster of strong and painful

---

31. Baum, *op. cit.*

32. Baum, *op. cit.*

33. For some people, or in some situations, it is more like rage and depression.

emotions, he begins to go into the final stage of grieving, which is that of acceptance.[34] It is with this more mature acceptance that we are bigger and better inside, more able to live in the world as it really is, and we grow and mature.

Adopt a paradigm shift

This realization, with its subsequent grieving reaction, will inevitably lead to real intrinsic change. Dorothy changed when she gave up the Wizard, and you, too, will change every time you give up one of your wizards. Your view of yourself, others, the world, your body, wealth, romance – all of this will change. You will then develop new, less idealized and more realistic ways of seeing yourself and the world you live in.

The funny thing is that people who go through this process are, in a paradoxical way, more happy and content. One reason for this is that they are more realistic about life, their work, themselves, their family, time, money, aging and their appearance.

After the defrocked Wizard left the Land of Oz in his air balloon, Scarecrow took his place. "The Scarecrow was now the ruler of the Emerald City and although he was not a Wizard the people were proud of him."[35] It is truly a paradigm shift to have a healthy thinking, reality-based Scarecrow rule you rather than a magical-thinking wizard. Let us take a look at some of the ingredients that go into a paradigm shift.

The elements of the new paradigm include:[36]

- **Personal responsibility.** Eventually and essentially our inner happiness is ours to find and keep. Dorothy did not realize at the time that it was the journey itself that made her strong and

---

34. If acceptance comes first, or too soon, it is not real grieving.

35. Baum, op. cit.

36. This excerpt is taken from an unpublished work by Sam Alibrando, Ph.D. and Alan Hedman, Ph.D.

successful. Rather than a free handout from a humbug Wizard, it was developing Scarecrow, Tin Man and Lion that brought her thinking, heart and courage. It was not and never would come from some magical wizard.

- **Courageously living in reality**. When it comes to success, there are no wizards, there are only courageous people living honestly in the world. Even though some people can at times change reality, we can never beat it. Wizards are an attempt to take a shortcut – the easy route – but in reality there are no shortcuts. Whenever you try to trick or cheat reality, you (or someone else, like your family or organization) will have to pay.[37]

"But how about my courage?" asked the Lion anxiously.

"You have plenty of courage, I am sure," answered Oz. "All you need is confidence in yourself. There is no living thing that is not afraid when it faces danger. True courage is in facing danger [reality] when you are afraid, and that kind of courage you have in plenty."[38]

- **Learning from experience**. In the movie, the Wizard gave Scarecrow a university diploma, Tin Man a testimonial in the shape of a heart and the Lion a metal of bravery; however,

Anything that the Wizard gave to the three companions was merely a token of what they had already received from the best tutor, experience.

---

37. Being realistic is not "selling-out." Being realistic does not mean that you are not forward thinking, innovative or a risk taker. It just means that you will have what it takes to change reality rather than fight it.

38. Baum, *op. cit.*

- Scarecrow learned wisdom from overcoming real life challenges; Tin Man learned to love by exercising his passions and compassions in all the challenges they faced and Lion learned courage from fighting – against fear itself – the dangers in front of him. Trial and error on the Yellow Brick Road is where we grow and change. There is no substitute for nor do we learn anything worth keeping other than what we learn from experience.

"Can't you give me brains?" asked the Scarecrow.

"You don't need them. You are learning something every day. A baby had brains, but it does not know much. Experience is the only thing that brings knowledge, and the longer you are on earth the more experience you are sure to get."[39]

This wonderful advice given by Oz came only after Dorothy angrily accused him of being a "very bad man." But he protested and defended himself by exclaiming, "Oh no my dear; I'm really a very good man; but I'm a very bad wizard." There really are no good wizards, only good men and good women.

Linda is in her late forties and has never been married. Up until only a few years ago, her wizard was, *"If only* I could find a husband ... *then* I would be happy." Subsequently, she went from one disappointing relationship to another. She was constantly depressed. I recently ran into Linda and she had changed. Her mood was up and her attitude positive. She was a different person from the woman I had known, and I wondered what had happened to bring about such a noticeable change.

She told me that she had gradually realized that her pursuit of "the man who will make her happy" was in vain. She had to go through a formidable grieving process to realize this. She became angry with God and life, and very sad as well. But over time, she came to accept her unmarried status and was then able to move into a variety of changes

---

39. Baum, *op. cit.*

in her life. She changed her career and adopted some new as well as neglected hobbies. She travels now and has cultivated new friends and interests that fulfill her and make her happy. She assured me that if a good man came along she would not resist, but she was no longer waiting on this *wizard* to make her happy. The paradigm of herself, men and romance – all that had changed. She had changed!

You will grow as well when you discover the fraudulent wizards in your life. Even though they promise you the world, they actually keep you from living freely in the world. Take it from the wizard himself, who said, "I am ashamed to say that I cannot keep my promises." Follow Dorothy's example and fire your wizard.

REFECTIONS

1. What things actually take up your energies, your thinking and pursuits? Make a list. Could any of these things be wizards in your life?

2. What people in your life have the most emotional control over you? Make a list. Could any of these people be a wizard in your life?

3. If these pursuits or people were to be lost today, what difference would that make in your life?

4. Integrate Your

SCARECROW, TIN MAN AND LION

"But then I should not have had my wonderful brains!" cried the Scarecrow. "I might have passed my whole life in the farmer's cornfield."

"And I should not have had my lovely heart," said the Tin Woodman. "I might have stood and rusted in the forest till the end of the world."

"And I should have lived a coward forever," declared the Lion, "and no beast in all the forest would have had a good word to say to me."

L. Frank Baum, *The Wonderful Wizard of Oz*

The third practice is the centerpiece and foundation of this book. Perhaps it is the centerpiece of *The Wonderful Wizard of Oz* as well. No characters in the story are more endearing and gripping than Scarecrow, Tin Man and Lion. I believe no characters in the story are as compelling psychologically as well.

Nearly a half a century after L. Frank Baum enriched the lives of countless children with *The Wonderful Wizard of Oz*, Karen Horney, M.D., enhanced the psychological world with her book, *Our Inner Conflicts,* which became a classic in its field. The book introduces the three primary ways people relate to others: by either *moving toward, moving against, or moving away* from others. Across the ocean in England – and independent of Dr. Horney – Wilfred Bion, M.D., used three different terms to describe how we emotionally "link" or *connect* to each other. He said that people interpersonally connect either through *love, hate* or *knowing*.

Although the terms differ, in essence, these two psychoanalytic giants, independently of each other, identified the three fundamental ways in which we interpersonally move or connect to others.[40]

Over the years, I have relied on these tripartite concepts to guide me as a therapist, a teacher and an organizational consultant. As I have worked with these concepts, I've gradually developed a model that I call the *Interpersonal Triad*.[41] The Interpersonal Triad is strongly confirmed throughout psychoanalytic literature as well as outside of psychoanalysis, in other places such as in philosophy, religion, literature and even pop culture.[42] But what does all this have to do with the Wizard of Oz?

The ideas of Karen Horney followed L. Frank Baum's *The Wonderful Wizard of Oz* by roughly half a century. My epiphany in connecting the two came in another half-century. It was a chance observation of children watching a video of *The Wizard of Oz* when it hit me: there they were – all three of them – and in, of all places, a children's story.

---

40. Horney's moving-toward is the same as Bion's *love*, moving-against is the same as *hate*, and in order to *know* something you have to move-away.

41. In previous editions I referred to the model as the *Interpersonal Triangle*.

42. Support for the concept of Horney's three movements and Bion's three links exists outside psychological literature. Examples of the Interpersonal Triad can also be found in organizational theory, popular culture and religion. Consider the following *Serenity Prayer:*

> God grant me the serenity to accept the things I cannot change (moving-toward)
> Courage to change the things I can (moving-against) and
> Wisdom to know the difference (moving-away).

Now a mainstay in Anonymous recovery programs, it was originally written by Reinhold Niebuhr in 1926.

Early in her journey Dorothy meets three companions – Scarecrow, Tin Man and Lion. Each of these companions has some characteristic that is underdeveloped and in need of fulfillment. Each joins Dorothy to find the Wonderful Wizard of Oz who will presumably give them those things that they lack. As it turns out, the Wizard has little to give them that they have not developed themselves along the Yellow Brick Road.

Let's look at the analogy in terms of Bion's links and Horney's movements. Remember Tin Man who cares about having a heart? He represents "love," or "moving toward." Lion, who battles for courage, represents "hate," or "moving-against." Finally, Scarecrow, obsessed with having a brain, symbolizes knowing, or "moving away."

These three comrades – Scarecrow, Tin Man and Lion – represent three ways we move interpersonally. They symbolize three key ways we constructively *connect* or destructively *disconnect* with other people. How well you develop Scarecrow, Tin Man and Lion in your life will determine how successful you will be in your relationships.

Just as we need to learn how to navigate the three dimensions of the physical world (height, width and depth) with balance and coordination, we need to learn how to navigate the three dimensions of the interpersonal world as well.

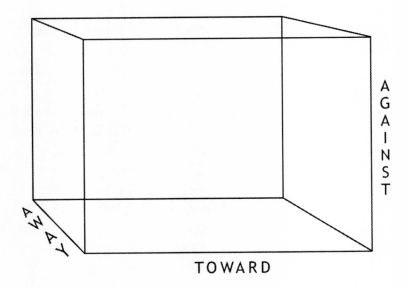

Figure 1. The three dimensions of the interpersonal world.

We learn how to navigate the interpersonal world when we are young. By the time we reach adolescence most of our *interpersonal habits* are strongly established, if not automatic. And to some extent, we all have relational patterns that are ineffective, especially when we are challenged by stressful interactions. So when our boss, spouse or child behaves in a disturbing way, we often and automatically can either get angry too fast, submit to soon or just emotionally disconnect.[43] Although we can still learn to move more positively through the interpersonal world, it takes a great deal of commitment. Typically we do not learn these complicated psychological skills when things are going well or when we are stuck in the repetitive Kansas of our life. We are much more likely to learn these tools when a twister picks up our life and drops us in the Land of Oz.

---

43. Negative Lion, Tin Man and Scarecrow, respectively. There will be more to come on this later in the chapter and in Appendix I.

The best place to learn Tin Man heart, Lion courage and Scarecrow knowing is just like where Dorothy did it, on the Yellow Brick Road.

In the next section, we will examine each of the three *companions*. Then we will look at how fear and anger bring about a negative expression of each companion, followed by how a positive coordination, or "synergy," is the answer to the dis-integration due to fear and anger. Finally we will learn from Dorothy's example how to bring about positive change using our three "companions."[44]

Loving Tin Man
(Moving Toward)

Tin Man wanted a *heart* so that he could *love*. Tin Man corresponds to moving toward or *love* – the human capacity to nurture and care for others and to be receptive to and dependent on others.[45]

If it were not for moving toward, society would be entirely different. Human beings would be amoral and ruthless. The world would be a perpetually dangerous place to live, without rules or regard for others.[46] "To love others as you love yourself" would be neither golden nor a rule.

---

44. For reasons of simplicity, from this point forward, I will mostly refer to Karen Horney's movements, instead of Wilfred Bion's links. I have the deepest respect for the work of Dr. Bion, however, most people seem to identify better with Horney's language.

45. The Tin Man represents what Carl Jung called the *anima,* or feminine, part of the human personality.

46. To the extent that the world is dangerous and without regard for others, that is the extent to which we fail at realizing the positive expression of Tin Man.

Tin Man (moving-toward) is psychologically oriented toward the OTHER.

Tin Man is concerned with what we *give to* the Other. It involves our interest in listening to and caring for the Other. A parent moves toward a child by nurturing and encouraging him or her. A lover moves toward the beloved with physical affection, erotic tenderness or selfless giving. A supervisor moves toward her subordinates by listening to their needs and ideas. An employee moves toward his employer by putting his whole heart into a project. A society moves toward its people by caring for the less fortunate.

There is a wonderful story in the book where the Tin Woodman accidentally steps on an insect.

> *Once indeed, the woodman stepped upon a beetle that was crawling along the road, and killed the poor little thing. This made the woodman very unhappy, for he was always careful not to hurt any living creature; and as he walked along he wept several tears of sorrow and regret ...*

In this story we see the profound moral aspect of moving toward. We see the regard for every other living thing.

Tin Man is also concerned with *dependency*: what we need *from* the Other. Dependency is scary for most people. When dependency works, we get our genuine needs met. A baby needs to be held and fed; a child may need to be helped with homework or guided through an emotionally difficult situation; a partner needs to be supported and cared for. An employee needs to be given guidance, to feel equipped to do the job and to be listened to and appreciated; an employer needs to receive feedback and input on projects and be given an honest day's work. The poor and disadvantaged need help to get back on their feet in order to become self-sufficient and successful.

Tin Man clearly represents dependency. He has to be oiled regularly or he rusts and seizes up. This is certainly the case for Tin Man aspects of our personalities. We need to be "regularly oiled" to keep us going.

"Did you groan?" asked Dorothy.

"Yes," answered the tin man; "I did. I've been groaning for more than a year, and no one has ever heard me before or come to help me.

"What can I do for you?" she enquired, softly, for she was moved by the sad voice in which the man spoke.

"Get an oil-can and oil my joints.... If I am well oiled I shall soon be all right again ..."

Katie grew up in a home with very immature parents. Attempts to be dependent on her parents were met with neglect, if not outright contempt. She eventually gave up on ever being able to depend on anyone. As an adult, she was frozen or "rusted" emotionally in many aspects of her life. It was only after many years of hard work in therapy that she began to let herself become vulnerable again. At first she had to let me "oil" her immobilized emotional joints with unconditional regard and acceptance. Later, she was able to let others do the same for her.

Courageous Lion
(Moving-Against)

Lion wanted **courage** so that he could **rule**. Lion represents moving-against, the human capacity to govern and control.[47] As much as Tin Man *love* characterizes being human, so also does Lion *aggression*.

---

47. Wilfred Bion uses the term "hate" to represent this capacity. Most people I encounter hate the word "hate."

Deep inside the limbic system of our midbrain, along with our capacity for passion and love, is also our instinct for aggression.[48]

Moving-against Lion is the basis of competition. It is "me vs. you;" it is "us vs. them." It is about being the winner, not the loser. It's about coming out on top, being number one, going to the head of the class, and experiencing the thrill of victory, whether the competition is Democrats vs. Republicans, Coke vs. Pepsi or the Dodgers vs. the Giants. Sometimes it is a competition within ourselves to accomplish a task, such as losing a few pounds or getting regular exercise. Lion fights the "good" fight and the "bad" fight. Lion just spoils for a fight. Where Tin Man centers on the Other ...

The psychological orientation or focus of moving-against Lion is on the SELF.

The "Self" could simply be about the first person singular, "I." However, it can also involve the "we" (or corporate identities), such as our family, our company, our neighborhood, our race, our team, our nation or our religion.

If it were not for moving-against Lion, human beings would not have the ambition to advance. We would all be obnoxiously agreeable and without any distinction, like a herd of lambs rather than a respected lion or lioness.

"All the other animals in the forest naturally expect me to be brave, for the Lion is everywhere thought to be the King of Beasts."[49] Lion (moving-against) is about being king or queen of your own forest.[50]

---

48. Lion represents what Carl Jung calls the *animus* or masculine side of the personality.

49. Baum, *op cit.*]

50. It is interesting that in the book, after Dorothy heads back to Kansas, Lion is given rule over an entire Kingdom of beasts in the Grand Old Forest over the hill from the Hammerheads. (The Hammerheads were one of many enemies that Dorothy and her crew had to face on their journey that did not make it into the movie.)

Most people are happy with a moderate expanse of domain. They like to be in charge of certain aspects of their life, such as freedom to work, or to raise a family in relative safety or to enjoy personal autonomy. Others want an enormous piece of forest – they are not happy unless they control everyone and everything around them. Still others give up any claim on forest real estate and offer themselves to the highest bidder. Which are you?

Lion has to do with *self-protection* as well. This is the ability to set and maintain adequate boundaries. Throughout history, people have had to protect themselves from intruders invading their land and taking their possessions. However, boundaries are also psychological and interpersonal in nature. Lion protects these interpersonal and psychological boundaries.[51]

Martha's mother calls her almost every morning, something that Martha especially dreads. During the calls, her mother dominates the conversation. Martha spends half an hour listening to her mother's negativity and never-ending list of worries. She wouldn't answer the phone if she thought she could get away with it – without a reprimand from her mother later on. Martha is afraid to set a boundary with her mother. She is afraid that her mother will be hurt – and angry – should she cut her phone calls short. Just like the Cowardly Lion, Martha is afraid to move-against.

For most people, having to confront others is an unpleasant, even terrifying, task. People will often go to extremes to avoid a conflict. They are afraid of being emotionally injured or injuring the other. Moving-against Lion involves the ability to confront another person to protect yourself and your interests.

---

51. If you are interested in the topic of boundaries, the reader is directed to the book *Boundaries* by Henry Cloud and John Townsend.

Knowing Scarecrow
(Moving-Away)

Scarecrow wanted a *brain* so that he could *think*. *Thinking* here means the psychological ability to take a step back in order to objectively look at things. It involves the capacity to move outside of a situation long enough to see it in an impartial, yet fresh, manner. Thinking is the ability to "move-away" from something in order to *know* it better. It is the ability to be psychologically and emotionally separate.[52] It is the ability to know.

> *When Dorothy presently asked him a question, the Tin Woodman could not open his mouth, for his jaws were tightly rusted together. He became greatly frightened at this and made many motions to Dorothy to relieve him, but she could not understand. The lion was also puzzled to know what was wrong. But the Scarecrow seized the oil-can from Dorothy's basket and oiled the Woodman's jaw, so that after a few moments he could talk as well as before.[53]*

Thinking or knowing, as I use it here, does not mean intelligence. Just because a person has a high IQ does not mean that he can "move-away" from emotionally charged situations and become reflective. There are many intelligent people who do not think.[54] At some time or another, we have all worked with people who were very skillful in their own area of expertise but could not "think" in emotionally charged situations. Thinking is not related to how many facts someone knows or even how logical someone can be. It has to do with the ability to endure a situation, and *not react* to it, allowing time to consider the situation from a fresh or more objective viewpoint.

---

52. In this way, thinking and moving-away are the same.

53. Baum, *op. cit.*

54. Very often, in fact, people who have extraordinary intelligence use it in place of thinking.

If it were not for Scarecrow, the world would be entirely different. There would be no consciousness or self-reflection. There would be no self-control. We would merely react and act out our lust or hatred. There would be neither science nor art, but only impulsivity and reactivity.

One of the key aspects of Scarecrow is *self-awareness*. Self-awareness is one of the more important ingredients in mental health and interpersonal effectiveness. It is a key component of what is referred to as emotional intelligence.[55] Certainly all of us at some time or another are unaware of what is going on psychologically. Yet there are some people who are nearly blind to who they are, how they feel or what motivates them. I personally find this type of person one of the hardest types of people to relate to. They can often see faults in others – real or imagined – but are blind to their own vulnerabilities or shortcomings. Scarecrow allows us to see ourselves more objectively and without that most disabling emotion, *shame*.[56]

If Tin Man is centered on the Other and Lion is focused on the Self, then

Scarecrow is psychologically oriented to Neither (Self nor Other).

Scarecrow wants to step out of the orbit of Other and Self in order to be unaffected, aware and objective. Dorothy's Scarecrow often boasts that he feels neither pain nor hunger; he can't be hurt because he is made of straw. The Scarecrow part of us is neither hurt nor offended.

I work with many executives who are reactive and short-tempered. Daniel is a brilliant businessman who often took things personally and

---

55 The reader is directed to the writings of Daniel Goleman on "emotional intelligence."

56 You can see the important place of "seeing" in the following excerpt: "After an hour or so the light faded away, and they found themselves stumbling along in the darkness. Dorothy could not see at all; and the Scarecrow declared he could see as well as by day. So she took hold of his arm and managed to get along fairly well." [Baum, *op cit.*]

then reacted with a strong show of force – so much so that others were in constant fear of him. Morale in his team was very low. In our executive coaching sessions, we would work on strengthening his Scarecrow side. We talked about trying to emotionally move-away from sensitive situations and to "count to ten" before he said or did anything. We tried to identify the triggers that would set him off in order to give him time to *think* about how he wanted to respond. As a result, he regained a great deal of self-control – not to mention respect from those who worked for him. Morale improved remarkably.

Feelings, Failings, Fears and Fight

I have introduced our three companions and the movements they represent. Now let's look at the feelings, failings (or negative effects), fears and fight (anger) associated with each of these movements.

Feelings and affects

Each relational movement has its own set of emotions. Tin Man involves the "soft" feelings such as love, sadness, passion and desire. After all, Tin Man frequently weeps. Tin Man involves feeling vulnerable; it inevitably leads to pain and hurt. If you love someone or something, you will be hurt. Count on it.

Lion entails the "hard" feelings such as anger, initiative, revenge, persistence, impatience and envy. If Tin Man encompasses being hurt, Lion involves feelings of hurting. If moving-toward is the affect of being vulnerable, moving-against is the affect of being invincible. The lion is an animal of intimidation and power. I recently visited a zoo where I had the opportunity to experience the awesome roar of a fully-grown lion. It was a powerful and commanding sound. It clearly sent the message, "Don't mess with me."

Where Tin Man (moving-toward) involves soft feelings and Lion (moving-against) involves hard feelings, Scarecrow (moving-away) involves *no feelings*; it is void of feeling, neither hard nor soft, neither hurt nor hurting. In the book version, *The Wonderful Wizard of Oz*, Scarecrow often talks about not needing anything. He does not eat and he does not sleep. He often talks about not feeling any pain; after all, he is "stuffed with straw." This is the very nature of moving away; it is without emotion. Where Tin Man and Lion probably abide in the limbic system – the emotional mid-brain, Scarecrow probably abides in the prefrontal cortex – the thinking and judging part of the brain.

Failures and effects

A movement – whether toward, against or away – seldom has a neutral effect. Most often the interpersonal movements in a relationship have either a positive or negative effect.[57] When I talk about changing for the better when life gives you its worst I am, of course, emphasizing the positive effects of each movement, which I will discuss in the next section on synergy. However, one must acknowledge that each of these movements can also have a negative, if not destructive, effect on others and oneself.

When Dorothy first meets each of her companions, she finds them in their negative position. Scarecrow, for example, is isolated and alone in the cornfield. As you recall, the positive expression of Scarecrow is his ability to be objective, to think and have self-control. The negative expression of this movement is when someone moves away *too much*. This is how we find Scarecrow: isolated, alone and ineffective. I once worked with Sid, a senior level executive who was a very good strategist and big-picture man but would frustrate his partners because they never knew what he was thinking or how he felt. He often withheld his input until the very end and was very stingy with compliments. He was like Scarecrow out there in the field.

Mary's husband was a source of constant frustration to her. He did not like anything that was in the least bit feeling-oriented. Anytime she

---

57. This idea of negative and positive effect will be covered in greater detail in Appendix I.

would bring up an emotionally charged issue, he would retreat into his inner "cornfield" by becoming emotionally disconnected until he could literally escape into another room.

When Dorothy first meets Tin Man, he is frozen and totally dependent. The positive expression of moving toward is seen in a person who cares for other people and who is able to realistically depend on others for needs that they cannot meet for themselves. The negative expression of this movement, however, is in someone caring and depending *too much* for his own good (and the good of the other). These are people who are too selfless, too compliant, too needy and too emotionally hungry and are what we have come to call "codependent."

Harry manages his work team by being "nice" and likeable. Those who work under him can talk him into almost anything and he is frightened of conflict and interpersonal friction. Tammy is the same way toward her husband and children. Any thought that she might have quickly evaporates in deference to a differing opinion within the family. Her life orbits around her husband and child, neither of whom treats her very well.

When Dorothy first meets Lion, he is mean, cruel and hurtful to her and her friends. The positive expression of Lion has to do with healthy aggression, honesty, self-expression, taking initiative and self-protection. The negative expression is not so pretty. It has to do with rage, domination, exclusivity, prejudice, envy, selfishness and even rape and murder. Sometimes the negative expression of Lion is large and obvious, such as in cases of murder, spousal or child abuse, and deliberate illegal behaviors that hurt the financial and physical wellbeing of others. Its more common expression in relationships is in cases of people being arrogant, judgmental, selfish, envious and controlling.

Linda treated the people who worked for her with disrespect if not disdain. She was demeaning, critical and sarcastic to her support staff. She was arrogant and cutthroat with her peers and was suspicious and highly offended by her supervisor's suggestion that she receive executive coaching for her negative behavior.

Fears and anxiety

St. Paul of Tarsus was a key leader in the early Christian Church. He wrote a letter to his apprentice, Timothy, who was the head pastor of the church in Ephesus. Apparently Timothy was having some interpersonal problems. In the letter, Paul wrote that Timothy was not given a spirit of fear or anxiety but a spirit of power, love and a sound mind.[58] In this short admonition, St. Paul clearly identifies all three movements or companions: power (Lion), love (Tin Man) and sound mind (Scarecrow). The thing that I find most interesting about this, however, is the first part about fear and anxiety.

Anxiety corrupts and distorts the interpersonal movements. It makes power nasty; it makes love weak; and thinking, indifferent.

Nineteen centuries later, Sigmund Freud would express a similar idea that anxiety is at the root of neurosis.[59]

Each of these movements has a *fundamental fear* or *anxiety* associated with it. Scarecrow (moving-away) has the fear of abandonment and loss connected to it. In the book, when Dorothy first finds him, he states that "[The Farmer] set me up on a tall stick … and left me alone. I did not like to be deserted this way … it was a lonely life …" The fear associated with Scarecrow is the fear of aloneness, neglect and abandonment. Scarecrow is afraid of being emotionally and relationally disconnected. It is the fear related to being psychologically separate. It is the nightmare of not belonging. It is the dread of being neither liked nor disliked … of not being paid attention to at all.

---

58. (II Timothy 1:7)

59. Many other psychoanalysts would offer a similar idea. In fact, Karen Horney, who coined the terms moving-toward, moving-against and moving-away in her book *Our Inner Conflicts*, bases her theory on this idea of anxiety as the root of neurosis.

In the book, the comrades encountered a river that prevented them from reaching the Yellow Brick Road on the other side. Scarecrow had the bright idea of making a raft and Tin Man quickly took on the task of cutting the wood. They made and then launched the raft and while out in the middle of the current, "Scarecrow pushed so hard on his long pole that it stuck fast in the mud at the bottom of the river, and before he could pull it out again, or let go, the raft was swept away and the poor Scarecrow was left clinging to the pole in the middle of the river.... Of course this was a bad thing for the Scarecrow."[60] It is indeed a bad thing for our inner Scarecrow to be left alone or abandoned.

Bill annoys everyone on his work team. He is always talking. People cringe when there is even a short silence in the discussion because they know that the next person to speak is going to be Bill whether he has something relevant to say of not. Worst of all, Bill doesn't realize he does this. Bill cannot move-away. He does not stop to think, so afraid is he of being separate and not belonging, of being stranded out on a pole all alone.

The fear associated with Tin Man (moving-toward) is different. It is the fear of being weak and left at the mercy of another or of life itself. It is the fear of being helpless and vulnerable. Tin Man always falls at the mercy of the world around him. He weeps frequently. His tears make him rust, the rust renders him immobile, and his immobility leaves him vulnerable and dependent.

This is often the fear that I find among corporate executives. They are comfortable in being aggressive (Lion) and "unaffected" (Scarecrow) but are terrified of being "weak" or vulnerable (Tin Man). This line of thinking sometimes works in authoritarian-structured organizations – such as the military – where someone needs to take control. However, most organizations today are less authoritarian and depend on teamwork and collaboration. The leader who is uncomfortable with their Tin Man ends up being deficient in the social skills necessary for this type of work environment.

---

60. Baum, op. cit.

The fear associated with Lion (moving-against) is that of guilt and "being bad." Lion, when we first meet him, attempts to intimidate Dorothy and her companions.

> *Just as [Tin Man] spoke, there came a terrible roar, and the next moment a great Lion bounded into the road. With one blow of his paw he sent the Scarecrow spinning over and over to the edge of the road, and then he struck the Tin Woodman with his sharp claws. [And] the Woodman fell over in the road and lay still.*[61]

But when he chases Toto, Dorothy chastises him for being mean to a poor, defenseless little dog. "'Don't you dare to bite Toto! You ought to be ashamed of yourself, a big beast like you, to bite a poor little dog! ... You are nothing but a big coward.'" Lion becomes terribly upset over someone yelling at him. "'No one would think of biting such a little thing except a coward like me,' continued the Lion sadly."[62] A person who fears moving against is afraid of hurting someone. Yet it goes a step further. If you are bad, you also fear that someone will lash back at you. The fear of moving against is that you will hurt someone or something and possibly get hurt in return.

Connie was a very attractive and sweet person oriented toward getting people to like her. This was the basis of her self-esteem.[63] As a result, she attracted a lot of men, especially male doctors at the hospital where she was a nurse. Her problem was she couldn't say "*No!*" To her, saying "no" felt like a "mean thing" to do; it would hurt their feelings. She was afraid to employ Lion (move-against) and set boundaries for herself. This led to many complicated work situations, lower job satisfaction and several very bad dates.

---

61. Baum, *op cit.*

62. Baum, *op. cit.*

63. This is an example of the negative expression of moving-toward.

Anxiety makes us lopsided

When we are beset with fear or anxiety we are more likely to become lopsided in how we interact, especially if the situation is tense.[64] For example, we might react to someone we are in conflict with in anger and cold indifference and not be able to empathize or accept our part in the conflict (negative Lion and Scarecrow without any good Tin Man).

We become lopsided when, because of anxiety, we underplay a positive expression of one companion and as a result overplay the negative expression of the other companions.

This generally results in a negative interaction, distortion, imbalance, ineffectiveness, poor communication and sometimes-harmful outcomes. Think of a lopsided tripod with one short leg and an off-balance camera on top.

When Dorothy goes before the Wizard in the Emerald City for the first time she is overtaken with fear and anxiety. As a result, she under-emphasizes the positive expression of moving away (thinking on her feet) and moving against (courage) and overemphasizes the negative expression of moving toward: She becomes weak, vulnerable and super-submissive. She is lopsided. You might argue, "Who wouldn't react this way to someone so frightening?" I agree. However, after Dorothy returns from melting the Wicked Witch of the West and the Wizard refuses their wishes once more, she is able to think about what is happening and has the courage to confront him. And as a result the secret about his being a fraud is exposed. She is no longer helplessly submissive; she is no longer lopsided. Read how Baum depicted this in his book where Dorothy and her companions return after melting the witch:

---

64. Sometimes the experience of the anxiety or fear is consciously "felt"; however, very often the anxieties or fears are not conscious and all we see are the behaviors that follow.

"Dear me, ... how sudden! Well come back tomorrow, for I must have time to think it over," [said the Wizard]

"You've had plenty of time already," said Tin Woodman angrily.

"We shan't wait a day longer," said the Scarecrow.

The Lion thought it might be as well to frighten the Wizard, so he gave a large, loud roar, which was so fierce and dreadful that Toto jumped away from him in alarm and tipped over the screen that stood in a corner.... They saw standing in just the spot the screen had hidden, a little old man, with a bald head and a wrinkled face, who seemed to be as much surprised as they were.

This is the essence of most negative interpersonal behavior: anxiety makes us lopsided. In the example above, Bill is afraid to move away (Scarecrow). Because he is not easily able to take a step back, tolerate aloneness and waits his turn – he is thrown out of balance. He over-emphasizes Lion and Tin Man and becomes obnoxiously *enmeshed* or entwined with others. The executive who is loath to move toward (Tin Man) out of fear of appearing – or worse – feeling weak, will automatically be lopsided in his or her use of negative Lion (being controlling and harsh) and negative Scarecrow (being emotionally detached and indifferent). And finally there is Connie who is averse to being a nasty (Lion), and therefore unable to set appropriate boundaries. Because she could not naturally move against, her only recourse was to avoid people (negative Scarecrow), which she could not readily do at work. Hence she was prey to any who would enter her domain (negative Tin Man).[65]

Table 1 compares the three companions based on positive and negative expressions, inherent feelings as well as the underlying fear related to each.

---

65. For more on lopsidedness, see Appendix I.

Table 1. Comparison of the Three Companions

Companion	Positive Expression	Negative Expression	Feeling	Fear of
Tin Man	Care, concern, empathy, "healthy dependency"	Compliant, inferior, sensitive, "unhealthy dependency"	Soft feelings, warmth, caring, love, fear	Being weak and vulnerable
Lion	Courage, assertive-ness, honesty, protective-ness	Hostility, rage, exploitation, hate, prejudice	Hard feelings, anger, resolution, envy, hate	Being "bad" and getting hurt back
Scarecrow	Objectivity, enduring, self-aware-ness & self-control	Emotionality disconnected, indifferent, avoids, isolates	No feelings, unaffected, objective	Being alone, abandoned, not belonging

Fear and anger

A brief word about anger is in order. There are theorists who believe that most if not all anger actually originates from fear. Others, however, believe that anger can be an original feeling. Whichever the case, it is important to acknowledge that anger can have a similar negative effect on the companions. Anger also corrupts and distorts the movements. It too makes power, nasty; love, weak;[66] and thinking, detached.

---

66. A good example of anger making love weak is what we call passive-aggressiveness; another example is when people become "martyrs."

If fear and anger are so deadening and deadly to our inner Scarecrow, Lion and Tin Man, what can we do? We need to do what Dorothy did and build an effective inner team through synergy.

Synergy

Synergy comes from the Greek word *synergos,* meaning, "working together." It is defined as the *integration* of two or more agents – in this case, three – so that their combined or cooperative effect is actually greater than the sum of their individual effects. When our three companions work together in a collaborative and positive fashion, not only does the quality of all three go up but also their ability to work together improves. The quality of the interpersonal connection reaches new levels. People change for the better.

One reason for this is because when the three companions work together, each corrects or modifies the other. For example, the Lion side cannot be too mean; it is corrected by Tin Man's regard and concern for the Other and Scarecrow's self-control and objectivity. Tin Man is never so weak and helpless because Lion will not give up his or her rule and Scarecrow can think on his feet. Scarecrow will never be so emotionally detached or relationally isolated because Tin Man and Lion will always pull him into an emotional and interpersonal orbit.

Even though they appear to be contradictory, the companions really do make a great team!

Dorothy needs the combined effect of *all three* of her companions. By the time that Dorothy reaches the witch's castle in the film, her three companions are starting to work more like a team. Tin Man is passionate to save Dorothy, Scarecrow has ideas on how to do it and, Cowardly Lion is starting to show some nerve. When the positive aspect of each companion starts to work together, synergy begins to take place and

Dorothy is ready to do one of the most difficult tasks of her journey, melting a witch.

Another example of synergy comes from a team that played in the 1980 Olympic Games. Man for man, the amateur U.S. Hockey team was inferior to the Russian team made up of professional players. However, through synergy, they worked together to transcend to a new level of effectiveness, enough to beat the Russians and then go on to win the gold medal.

There is a great example of synergy from Baum's book. Dorothy was traveling with her companions through a "dark and gloomy" forest. They reach a section of the Yellow Brick Road that was blocked by a sizeable gulf.

> *So they sat down to consider what they should do, and after serious thought the Scarecrow said,*

> *"Here is a great tree, standing close to the ditch. If the Tin Woodman can chop it down, so that it will fall to the other side, we can walk across it easily."*

> *"That is a first-rate idea," said the Lion. "One would almost suspect you had brains in your head, instead of straw."*

> *The Tin Woodman set to work at once, and so sharp was his axe that the tree was soon chopped nearly through. The Lion put his strong front legs against the tree and pushed with all his might, and slowly the big tree tipped and fell with a crash across the ditch, with it tip branches on the other side.*

> *They had just started to cross this queer bridge when a sharp growl made them all look up, and to their horror they saw running toward them two great beasts with bodies like bears and heads like tigers....*

> *"Quick!" cried the Scarecrow. "Let us cross over."*

So Dorothy went first, holding Toto in her arms; the Tin Woodman followed, and the Scarecrow came next. The Lion, although he was certainly afraid, turned to face the Kalidahs, and then he gave so loud and terrible a roar that Dorothy screamed ... without stopping an instant the fierce beasts also began to cross the tree, and the Lion said to Dorothy,

"We are lost, for they will surely tear us to pieces with their sharp claws. But stand close behind me, and I will fight them as long as I am alive."

"Wait a minute!" called the Scarecrow. He had been thinking what was best to be done, and now he asked the Woodman to chop away the end of the tree that rested on their side of the ditch. The Tin Woodman began to use his ax at once, and, just as the two Kalidahs were nearly across, the tree fell with a crash into the gulf, carrying the ugly, snarling brutes with it, and both were dashed to pieces on the sharp rocks at the bottom.[67]

This is a great example of synergy. All three companions worked together, using the best of each attribute: Scarecrow's wisdom in the face of danger, Tin Man's servant's attitude and, yes, Lion's outstanding courage and nerve. None could have stood on his own effort; they had to work together like a team.

The same is true with our inner Scarecrow, Tin Man and Lion: When they work together, each companion's quality improves the others and we become more whole and effective people.

How We Change

How we change is complex. As it pertains to the three companions, however, let us take our lead from Dorothy. When we first meet Dorothy's

---

67. Baum, *op. cit.*

three inner companions they are in a negative position. Scarecrow is isolated and detached, Tin Man is weak and vulnerable and Lion is mean, even cruel. All of them know (self-awareness) that something is undeveloped in their characters. As they start to travel the Yellow Brick Road, each of their weaknesses is tested through different challenges. Gradually, the companions face these weaknesses and fears and deal with them.

Through experience – and only through experience – did Dorothy's companions grow and change.

The movement that has the most fear connected to it at any given time becomes the weak link in the interpersonal transaction.[68] As we know, a chain is no stronger than its weakest link. Even as a child I thought that Dorothy's weak link was the "cowardly" Lion. Even though he is mean and cruel when we first meet him,[69] Lion throughout most of the rest of the movie shows his lack of courage and healthy aggression. It is only when Lion finds his nerve toward the end of the film that synergy takes place among the companions, and they reach a new level of effectiveness. It is then that Dorothy can confront and melt her Witch as well as unmask a fraudulent wizard. With her companions integrated, her witch melted and her wizard defrocked, Dorothy was now ready to go home – as a new and better person. The hero's journey completed – mission accomplished!

The elements that are necessary for Dorothy are the same elements that we need in order to grow and be more effective. The guidelines for enhancing synergy among our inner companions is simple but, as usual, not easy:

- Recognize and own when we are expressing negative aspects of a companion;

---

68. I refer to this as the *missing movement*. See the previous discussion of lopsidedness and anxiety as well as Appendix I for more details.

69. The negative manifestation of moving-against.

- Recognize and own our weak link companion and resulting lop-sidedness (and the underlying fear or anger);

- Attempt to strengthen and integrate the positive expression of that weak link companion;

- Act on the synergy. When you do the above, synergy will take place. Do not resist it as it takes place.

- Practice this until it becomes a part of you.

My job as a therapist and as an organizational consultant is to help people change. When I present workshops on communication or conflict resolution, I first introduce the *Interpersonal Triad*, the three companions. I discuss the positive and negative effects of each. After people become familiar with the concepts, I help them identify the weak link on which they need to work in a given context (e.g., as a leader at work or with their spouse at home). We find short-term and long-term solutions to strengthen the weak link companion. As they improve their weak link companion they improve in their *overall* communication and interpersonal skills on the job and at home. (After they improve in this one area, generally a new weak link companion will emerge for them to work on. From there, the growth process moves forward.)

Here is how it worked for Bill from our earlier example. Bill annoyed everyone in his work team because he dominated and talked too much. When I coached Bill, I first helped him see that his negative expressions of Lion (dominating the discussions) and Tin Man (wanting to be liked) was primarily due to his anxiety around his weak link or *missing movement* – Scarecrow. I explained that when we have anxiety in one movement, it will manifest as negative expressions in the other movements. I explored with him the meaning of the anxiety and what generally triggered it. After we got a good enough understanding of his weak link, we came up with some ways to positively express Scarecrow in team meetings.[70] When he was able to do this in the team meetings he soon experienced the positive results of his new behaviors in how he felt about himself and in how others related to him. We then set up a plan to establish this new behavior as a habit.

Just as it worked for Dorothy and Bill, this "tool" can work for you. If you learn to let your Scarecrow think, your Tin Man care and you Lion roar, together as an effective synergistic team, you will be more effective in any and all of your relationships. I guarantee it!

(If you would like to know more about the three companions, I highly recommend that you read Appendix I, where these ideas are discussed in more detail.)

---

70. For example, he spoke only every third time he had the impulse to speak; he took notes and developed summary statements; he asked the group to ask him for his opinion when they were ready to hear it.

REFLECTIONS

1. Of Dorothy's three companions, which do you like the best and why? Which do you like the least and why? What does this tell you about yourself?

2. When you get upset with your spouse (partner, boy/girlfriend, parent, roommate, etc.), are you more likely to be a mean Lion, a frozen Tin Man or a detached Scarecrow? Which companion do you have the hardest time expressing with your upset partner or friend? What do you fear would happen if you expressed the positive aspect of that companion?

3. When you get upset with your boss (employee, client, vendor) are you more likely to be a mean Lion, a frozen Tin Man or a detached Scarecrow? Which companion do you have the hardest time expressing with your upset boss (employee, client, vendor)? What do you fear would happen if you expressed the positive aspect of that companion?

5. Melt Your WITCHES

The Witch had just stolen one of Dorothy's cherished shoes. This made her so angry that she picked up a bucket of water that stood near and dashed it over the Witch, wetting her from head to foot. And with that the wicked woman gave a loud cry of fear and began to shrink away.

"See what you have done!" she screamed. "In a minute I shall melt away."

L. Frank Baum, *The Wonderful Wizard of Oz*

And melt away she did. In the movie version, Dorothy is there with her loyal companions, face-to-face with her adversary. In a brave and loving attempt to save Scarecrow, she dowses water on the ugly hag, who melts like a cube of sugar in hot coffee. In the book (quoted above), it is only Dorothy and Lion who remain to face the wicked witch (Scarecrow and Tin Man were undone by the flying monkeys).[71] This time Dorothy in an attempt to rescue her cherished shoes soaks the "wicked woman" with a bucket of water, having the same result as with the witch in the movie – she melts away.

In the hero's journey, there is always something or someone the hero has to confront if not defeat in order to complete the journey. For

---

71. I find it interesting that when it finally came down to it, Dorothy only had Lion courage left to deal with the most dreaded witch.

Dorothy that someone was the Wicked Witch of the West.[72] I believe that the Wicked Witch symbolizes what we are afraid of in our life and need to confront if we are to grow and change. Our personal "witches" can be either internal or external. Examples of external witches might be a mean critical boss, a friend that continually annoys us, or an estranged family member.[73]

However, for our purposes, we will restrict our discussion to internal witches. Internal witches refer to the psychological aspects within us that are scary, unwanted, denied or otherwise avoided. This idea is by no means new. There are numerous examples of this in mythology, art, literature and movies. When Luke Skywalker, in the film *The Return of the Jedi*, is finishing his training as a Jedi Knight, he goes into a cave to face his ultimate fear. There, he struggles with – and finally unmasks – his archenemy, Darth Vader, only to find his own face under the mask. Like Luke Skywalker, our greatest "challenge" is always within ourselves.

I was giving a talk once to a group of single adults on the topic of finding a mate. I asked a question:

"What would have happened to Dorothy if she had never gone on her journey down the Yellow Brick Road?" I proceeded to answer my own question. "She probably would have married a self-centered and hostile man." After a moment of silence and stares from the audience, I continued. "You see, she would be attracted to her witch." I went on by stating that the witch represents a facet of Dorothy's personality that she denies and avoids – in this case Dorothy's selfish angry side.[74] Unless she dealt with her inner witch we would find her ten years later still affected by, attracted to and embroiled in aspects of her witch. If we observed her in

---

72. She also had many other challenges (more so in the book), not the least of which was her need to unmask the Great Wizard (see Chapter 3).

73. The way we deal with external witches is discussed in Chapter 4 and Appendix I, on the Three Companions.

74. I believe that Dorothy's witch in the movie is the negative expression of the Lion (or negative moving-against). As stated in Chapter 4, I believe that Lion was Dorothy's weakest link.

a room with several men, she would attract and be attracted to the one who was most like her inner witch, whether she realized it or not.

Most people understandably avoid their personal witches. They do it however, at a great cost. For they will be embroiled with their witch until they finally face her. Take another example. If you are terrified of being "weak," you will have to constantly be proving yourself to be strong. Without knowing it you might marry a "weak" spouse, overly react to perceived "weakness" in your children or surround yourself with ineffectual employees. That is until you finally and honestly face your inner fears – as Dorothy had to do in the story.

> *The man or woman who honestly faces himself or herself is truly the bravest of all human beings.*

I often hear people deny the opportunity to get professional counseling or executive coaching because they "do not need it." As if they are stronger than that. They see getting professional help in whatever form as a sign of weakness. They are deceiving themselves. People who fully and honestly engage in the process of facing themselves are the strongest and bravest people on earth.[75]

Carl Jung was a famous psychoanalyst who broke from the ranks of Freud to pursue his own very unique and popular course of analysis. Jung introduced an archetype[76] that he called the *shadow*. The shadow is the opposite side of the conscious personality. If we see ourselves as nice, the shadow will be mean; if we see ourselves as strong, the shadow will be weak; if we see ourselves as self-sufficient, our shadow side is dependent.

---

75. And they know that no one can face them self honestly without outside input and help (see Chapter 6 on Resources).

76. An archetype is something that serves as the model or pattern for other things of the same type. In Jungian psychology, it is an inherited memory represented in the mind by a universal symbol and often observed in dreams and myths – like the Wizard of Oz. Encarta® World English Dictionary © 1999 Microsoft Corporation.

Jung made a very discerning observation. He noted that the shadow embodies just those qualities that we dislike in other people. If you are in a staff meeting and you are *unusually* bothered by a colleague's forceful and non-empathic way of dealing with people, it is likely that this is the very side of your own personality that you are denying.

Jung noted a dilemma. The shadow side can be not only very destructive, but it also contains the vital forces of the personality. When one approaches the shadow, or the witch, one needs to proceed with great caution, because such a pursuit can be truly hazardous. On the other hand, one can't afford *not* to proceed, since *the shadow also contains the valuable resources for growth, survival, effectiveness and creativity.* I believe we have a lot to learn from Dorothy regarding this most important life task of facing our witches.

Three Categories of Witches

Witches can be grouped into three *categories*, using the three movements of the Interpersonal Triad. As you will recall, Scarecrow, Tin Man and Lion each had a negative or destructive side. These three negative expressions of Dorothy's companions provide like definitions for the categories of witches we ourselves face.

The "moving-against" witch

Perhaps the most common witch, and certainly the witch that Dorothy had to face in the movie, was the *moving-against* witch. This internal witch is selfish and hateful. If you remember, moving against in the positive form fosters healthy competition, honesty, and the discovery of the *courageous lion* within. But its ugly side is one of selfishness, domination, prejudice, hate, exploitation, and violence. It is the force behind sexual exploitation, political corruption, family violence, corporate greed and racism.

I consciously value equality, inclusion and diversity. I hate prejudice and bigotry. Yet at times I find myself reacting with bias against people who are different from me. I am shocked at myself when I make these automatic judgments against people. Yet, I cannot deny the side of my mind that can do this. The best that I can do at those moments is to humbly face the fact that I have a shadow side that is as ugly as Dorothy's *moving-against* witch.

The "moving-toward" witch

Although the moving-against witch is the most notorious, we can also be terrified by and deny our softer side as well. The healthy aspects of moving toward involve our positive regard for others and appropriate dependency on them. The witch version of moving toward, however, stems from both real or imagined vulnerability and weakness.

I once coached a manager of a midsized company who had an excellent business sense but was appalling when it came to relating to people. In fact, he was impossible to work with. He could not tolerate people who had any weakness or shortcoming. He would often refer to certain co-workers as "emotional invalids." Support staff would request transfers as soon as they could. As we began to work together, it was obvious that he was terrified of his *moving-toward* witch, that is, his own feelings of weakness and inadequacy. Whenever he saw these "scary" traits in others he would overreact to them, becoming critical, if not vicious. It was only after he began to own his own feelings of vulnerability and dependency that he began to temper his reactions to other people's demonstration of the same.

The "moving-away" witch

Finally, there is the *moving-away* witch. This is the hardest witch to detect but perhaps the most terrifying to experience. The positive expression of moving away is the ability to take a step back from an interpersonal or emotional situation in order to think clearly about it. The negative aspect of moving away is that of emotional and interpersonal detachment. The fear associated with this movement is fear of abandonment and isolation.

It has been said that children would rather be hit than ignored. This is true for many adults as well. Abandonment is one of the most rudimentary human fears.

> *This is neither the witch of hate nor the witch of neediness, it is the witch of nothingness – and she is as feared and as undesirable as any other witch.*

She is the witch of emptiness, the void and the gap. I cannot tell you how many people remain in very bad, if not destructive, relationships because of this witch. They are terrified of being alone.

Once, while I was facilitating a process group for organizational leaders, one of the group's members dominated the conversation. If there was a lull in conversation, he would talk; if someone said anything, he was always the next one to speak. Needless to say, he began to irritate everyone. At first he was accused of being controlling and stealing other people's time. What eventually came to the surface was that he had a *moving-away* witch. He could not tolerate silence, inactivity or what I like to call "the gap." To him, a gap in space and time was as scary and ugly as Dorothy's witch.

Three Ways We Experience *Bad* Witches

Now that we've identified the three general *categories* of witches, let's look at three different ways we experience witches: witches who are *truly bad, bad by intensity* and *bad by phenomenon*. There are many meanings for the word "bad." I use the term *bad* here as any real deficit or harmful behavior that is unwanted, scary or ugly. Let's start with the truly bad witch experience.

A truly bad witch

We refer to a witch as truly bad because they are, in fact, truly bad. Probably more often than we realize, we experience impulses that are truly violent, racist, selfish, greedy, lustful, weak or indifferent. If we exercise self-control, then these impulses remain in us only as latent thoughts and feelings.[77] However, when we are tired or careless, we may readily act on our impulses in varying degrees, often hurting others and ourselves in the process. These impulses are not aberrations, they are real and they are derived from these destructive inner witches.

We see evidence of truly bad "witchery" every day in the media coverage of current events. Politicians lie, drug addicts steal, business owners cheat, wealthy people don't share and gang bangers kill. Otherwise-considered-average citizens emotionally neglect their children, evade taxes, cheat on their spouse, and abuse alcohol. Books and movies are full of story lines containing greed, murder, lust and complicity. Along with stories of heroism, history is often an accounting of the effects of witches operating on a large social or political scale. All of these are examples of human interactions brought about by the truly bad witch.

Bad by intensity!

Sometimes a witch is not inherently bad, but rather is experienced as bad or ugly simply because it is *felt so strongly*. Emotion in and of itself is not wrong. Emotion is just emotion. The "truly bad" type of witch experience has to do with attitudes and impulses, whereas this second type of bad witch experience is about *magnitude* or *intensity*. For example, Pam is a very self-sufficient person who grew up in a home with a very needy and depressed mother. Whether at work or at home she seldom asks for help from other people who could otherwise be a resource for her. Pam met a young man with whom she was falling in love. Her feelings for

---

77. It takes a combined effort of Scarecrow to contain the impulses, Tin Man to have regard for how an impulsive behavior would affect another, and Lion to protect our own interests, to bring about "self control."

this man were strong, too strong for what she was used to. The mere strength of her need for him was scary and made her want to run from the relationship. In this case the feeling were not bad per se; instead it was the very strength and *intensity* of her feelings that was scary.

Of course it does not have to be love only; it could also be a moving-away feeling of aloneness and perhaps the most dreaded moving-against feeling of anger or hate. In most cases the emotional experience of the companion – whether Scarecrow, Tin Man or Lion – is not negative per se, but the "badness" comes from the mere intensity of the experience.

Tom Hanks played a character, in the movie *A League of Their Own,* named Jimmie Dougan, a washed-up, major league baseball player who ended up being the manager of an All American Girls' Baseball League team during World War II. In one scene he calls over one his players, Evelyn, who has just messed up a play for the umpteenth time. With trembling hands and tremulous voice he says, "I would … really appreciate it … if you … would work on that … play … by next season." All the time his eyes are wincing and his hands are shaking. Evelyn returns to the dugout while Dougan looks out onto the field, still trembling and grimacing in an effort to regain his composure. Jimmie Dougan's confrontation of the player was socially appropriate for the context; he did not attack her verbally or physically. Therefore it was not a "truly bad" witch that he encountered. However it was an emotionally scary experience by the sheer intensity of the feelings.

Bad by phenomenon!

The best way to define this type of witch is to give a quick example. Imagine you just got out of a horror movie about snakes. On the way home you are walking by a yard that has a hose lying in the grass. Out the corner of your eye, you see what you perceive to be a long green snake, but it's really just a garden hose. A surge of spine-chilling fear runs through your whole body. The reality is that the object is a green garden hose. However, you believe – by phenomenon – it's a green snake.

Many people have predisposed ideas that are strongly engraved in their mind. Because of these *paradigms*, they experience certain things as bad merely because they intrinsically *believe* that they are bad.

I know a woman who was raised in a home where the premise was "children should be seen and not heard." When she meets with her team leader at work she acts shy and reserved around him. The corporate environment in which she works supports openness between management and employees, but the very idea that she could – or even would – openly disagree with her boss feels *bad* to her. It is not truly bad, because no one is really hurt by it, nor is her disagreement by any means bad by intensity. But the *phenomenon* of its ugliness is embedded in her paradigm, her perceptions and beliefs that say it's bad.

It is important to know which type of witch experience we are having because it will determine how we go forward. If it is a "truly bad" witch, self-control is called for in the situation. If it is a witch by intensity, we need to ride out the emotional wave, knowing that it will eventually pass. And if it is a phenomenal witch, we need to correct our faulty assumptions and paradigms.

If we combine the three categories of witches – that correspond to the three companions – and the three different ways we experience witches, we can essentially delineate as many as nine personal witches. For example we could have real cruelty (a negative moving-against and "truly bad"), intense aloneness (moving-away and "intensity") or have perceived neediness (moving-toward and "phenomenon"). In any and all cases however, witches are scary. Most of us, like Dorothy, do not know how to deal with witches and often we use psychological strategies to avoid a bad witch experience that end up being more harmful than good. Let's look at some of those ways.

How Not to Deal with Witches

Regardless of what type, when we experience a witch, we are "not in Kansas anymore," we are in the Land of Oz. Therefore, any of the exit strategies (mentioned in Chapter 2) used to prematurely get out of the Land of Oz are ways by which we avoid dealing with witches. For example let's say that Michael is terrified of being alone. Instead of experiencing and dealing with his lonely witch, he escapes by manically overworking or getting drunk every night.[78] In doing this, he avoids an encounter with his witch.

In this section I would like to highlight three other common, yet harmful, strategies of evading witches. We can choose to *project out, dissociate from* or *identify with* the personal witches in our lives.

Projection

"Projection" is a moving-against strategy. Instead of facing our inner witch and taking ownership of her, we do something that psychologists have recognized for a long time. We project them. Projection is the psychological process by which we get rid of unwanted psychological experiences by seeing them in other people instead of in ourselves. We get rid of witches by projecting them onto others all the time. The manager noted above is a good example for how projection works. If you'll remember, he had a *moving-toward* witch. He was terrified of his strong feelings of dependency (bad by intensity). He saw his needs as weak and despicable (bad by phenomenon) and at times had real deficits in his skill set (truly bad). So instead of dealing with the Tin Man side of himself, he would *project* his own neediness onto the "emotional invalids" who worked for him. When something wrong happened, he blamed these employees for being weak and incompetent. In essence, he got rid of his "needy" witch, and instead saw it and reacted to it in his subordinates.

Projection is the basis of prejudice, racism and sexism. Throughout recorded history, one group of people has attributed to another group of people their own unwanted, frightening attitudes and traits. Then the group would either move away from or move against this other group. The Nazis are a good example. They projected their "inferiority witch"

---

78. Please see the first discipline, *The Land of Oz*, for more on this.

onto Jews, Blacks and Gypsies. This left *them* as the "superior race." Their first solution was to avoid or move away from them. They put them into ghettos. Their ultimate solution was to eliminate them from the face of the earth. This is a catastrophic and extreme example of what we do all the time in our own families, churches, companies and society.

Dissociation

Dissociation is a moving-away strategy. In psychology, we use the term "dissociate" to describe the experience of psychologically disconnecting from an emotionally charged situation. Everyone, at some point (and to differing extents), dissociates themselves from situations. When we are driving along the freeway and suddenly find ourselves at the bottom of our off-ramp without any idea how we got there, we have just experienced a mild case of dissociation. The extreme version of this happens in severe cases of child abuse, where the child who is being abused by an adult psychologically leaves the situation while his or her body remains to endure the assaults of the perpetrator.

When we encounter an inner witch, we often dissociate, or psychologically and emotionally disconnect. I notice this with clients when they get close to an inner witch; they often shift into a more detached state where their voice and emotions flatten. They dissociate. They avoid the witch – at least for the time being.

Identification

A less *logical* moving-toward solution to deal with witches follows the assumption that "if you can't beat them, join them." Sometimes we *become* the witch in order to avoid the direct and painful experience of the witch. People have observed that prisoners of war will sometimes take on the philosophy and behaviors of their captors. What happens if your captor is an internal witch? As odd as it seems, a person deals with the witch by becoming the witch. Growing up with a critical mother and an emotionally detached father, Greg never felt good about himself. He saw himself as defective and a failure. Where others might try to avoid this witch by overcompensating, blaming others or emotionally detaching, Greg identified with the "loser" witch. And despite seeming efforts to the contrary, he failed at mostly everything he did in spite of real talent and resources. Greg dealt with his witch by succumbing to her.

Before we move on to healthy ways to handle witches, let's consider a few important things about the power of witches. Whether they are really bad, or just psychologically strong, they are powerful and have real dynamic sway over people, families, organizations and society.

- **Witches become even more powerful when we avoid them**. Paradoxically the more you try to avoid them the stronger they get. So when you employ the strategies we mentioned above, not only do they not work, they can ironically strengthen the power of the witch.

- **Witches make us their slave**. After being commissioned to kill the Wicked Witch by the Wizard, Dorothy asked the Guardian of the Gate how to find her. "'That will be easy,' replied the man; 'for when she knows you are in [her territory] she will find you, and make you her slave.'" Whether we know it or not, we become slaves to our witches.

- **Witches feed off our fear.** As cancer feeds off blood, so do our personal witches get sustenance from our anxiety. The more we are consciously – or more importantly, unconsciously – afraid of them, the more power they have over us.

- **Witches have mono-vision.** Baum's Wicked Witch of the West had only one eye, yet that one eye was as "powerful as a telescope, and could see everything and everywhere." By virtue of having only one eye, Baum's witch had tunnel vision. If a witch takes over, all we see and feel comes from the witch's narrow

perspective. The wicked witch in the book got rid of Scarecrow
– the ability to think and have insight – as well as Tin Man – the
ability to care about others. Witches take over how we think and
feel. They put us under their spell. "'This is bad,' said the Tin
Woodman, 'for ... we shall be carried off into the country of the
Wicked Witch of the West, and she will *enchant* us and make us
her *slave.*'" [79]

So avoiding a witch, no matter how scary, is not the best way to man-
age the forbidding stuff inside us. How then should we handle the horrible hags within? Once again, we can follow the lead of our heroine,
Dorothy.

Proper Ways to Deal with Witches

*Our automatic tendency is to run toward wizards and
flee from witches. But if we want to change and grow,
we must learn to do exactly the opposite.*

If we want to change for the better when life gives us its worst, we
need to flee from our wizards and face our witches. In mythology, this
is invariably the quest of the hero. He or she must go into the dark and
forbidding forest, cave, or underworld and confront that which is the
most frightening.

The last thing Dorothy wants to do with her three companions is to
oppose that scary, green-faced hag on her own territory. However, she
and her companions are compelled by a higher purpose. And it is when
Dorothy deliberately and fully confronts the witch that the witch *melts.*
The same goes for us: When we face our inner witches, they melt.

A friend told a story of how she was wrongly confronted by a co-
worker. She told her therapist about this situation and the therapist invited

---

79. The italics are mine. All quotes are otherwise from L. Frank Baum, *The
Wonderful Wizard of Oz.*

her to speak all the voices that were in here mind. Some of the voices were those of scared young parts of herself that wanted to apologize – for a sin never committed – and appease the other person (negative Tin Man); another set of voices wanted to retaliate and put this person in her place (negative Lion). Finally the therapist asked her, "With all these voices that are yours, which one do you want to be 'Chairman of the Board' and take the lead?" My friend thought about it for a while and decided that she wanted the "adult" voice to take the lead. In this case the adult voice was the part of her that took a step back and decided to do nothing – to let it go (positive Scarecrow).[80] As a result, the antagonist had nothing to react to and the situation went away. The important lesson here was that my friend had to pay attention to all the voices – internal witches – first, before she was free to listen to the more "adult" (synergistic) part of herself.

I have consistently found that when we face our innermost fears, they melt a bit. They never seem to melt as much as Dorothy's witch in the story but they do lose some of the power they hold over us. When we confront them honestly and with vitality and truthfulness, they invariably get smaller.

There are four helpful things to keep in mind when we confront our personal witches.

Awareness

It is hard if not impossible to change and successfully go through a life-challenging twister without awareness. Awareness is defined as being conscious, and having or showing realization, perception or knowing. Awareness includes the mental experience of realizing something important about ourselves that we just didn't get before. Usually when this happens, some sort of emotional release or integration takes place.

---

80. Please note that she had to integrate the weak link – Scarecrow – in order to find the "adult" part of her self. Please see Appendix I for more on *Working the Triad*.

The "water" of awareness erodes the mean, wicked witch of the subconscious.

Witches do not like water. "Indeed, the old witch never touched water, not ever let water touch her in any way." You see witches *have no blood.* "The witch did not bleed … for she was so wicked that the blood in her had dried up many years before." [81] Early notions of witches held that because of their wickedness, witches' blood is completely dried up and they were maintained solely by magic. This makes them particularly vulnerable to water. Therefore, you can beat a witch by dousing her with water. I believe that shameless (or grace-filled) awareness is the water that melts our inner witches.

I observed this once when I was counseling Raymond. His eyes suddenly grew bigger. It was as if he'd seen something for the first time. He slowly started talking about things we had discussed many times before, but all of a sudden it started making sense to him. "I *believe* that I am inferior," he said. "I've always considered myself inferior … and that feels awful." He sat for a moment with a tear peeking from the corner of his eye. Then he continued, "My father always had to be 'one up' on me. He could never let me feel good about myself unless he was better." That was all he said for the next few moments.

Raymond faced a witch from his subconscious and by doing so it melted a little. After this experience, he started to exhibit more confidence, energy and productivity at work and was less intimidated by the employees he supervised. He faced a scary "bad" witch and she melted a little bit.

Fear is normal

"But how about my courage?" asked the Lion anxiously.

---

81. Baum, *op. cit.*

"You have plenty of courage," answered Oz. "There is no living thing that is not afraid when it faces danger. True courage is in facing danger when you are afraid, and that kind of courage you have."[82]

A certain amount of fear is normal – even healthy.

Being fearless has nothing to do with courage.

If you are not afraid when you face a witch, you are either not really facing a witch, or you are out of touch with reality.

Courage is a function of action, not emotion. I have a friend who went skydiving to celebrate his fiftieth birthday (don't ask me why). He tells of the terror he experienced when it was his turn. As he stood there in the open door of the airplane, with his parachute on, the instructor simply told him to "arch his back and jump" … and he did! Courage has to do with arching your back and jumping.

Dorothy had to jump, figuratively speaking. When she realized that she had to face the mean witch, she was afraid. But in spite of the fear, Dorothy arched her back and jumped. She committed herself to the dark forest and pointed herself in the direction of the witch. Whether our witch is a green-faced hag, an aggressive boss or a "needy" part of ourselves, it is normal to be afraid.

I once worked on a consulting project with an older colleague who was a powerful "lioness." She was a commanding woman who knew what she wanted and generally got her way. As strong as I can be, I often found myself automatically yielding to her in decisions that we had to make together (negative Tin Man). I would also withdraw and let her take the lead without much resistance (negative Scarecrow). At one time we came to an juncture where my needs were at cross-purposes with her interests. I had to act on my own behalf but knew how often I

---

82. Baum, *op. cit.*

had yielded to her and detached. I needed Lion.[83] I was afraid of having a confrontation with her. I was anxious to set the meeting, and then I was scared to speak my mind at the meeting. But just like Dorothy, I was compelled to do this for good cause. So knowing what I had to do, I *arched my back* and jumped. I phoned her and committed myself to an appointment. At the meeting I *arched my back* again and told her what I wanted to do. I was nervous the entire time, but with Lion taking the lead, supported by a reasonable Scarecrow and respecting Tin Man, we negotiated an equitable solution to the problem.

Three companions

Dorothy doesn't face her witch alone. She brings her three companions with her.[84] When we face our witches, we need to take along with us the attributes represented by the three companions:

- **We need Lion's courage.** Remember that courage has nothing to do with being fearless. Courage has to do with arching your back and jumping, in spite of the fear.

- **We need Tin Man's passion and purpose.** Dorothy is compelled by a higher purpose. Any healthy march into hell **has** to be for a heavenly cause. Tin Man's heart encompasses those "heavenly causes." Raymond, in the earlier example, marched into the "hell" of his negative self-image in order to be free of the burden of feeling inferior. He wanted to feel good about himself and he did not want to be pushed around anymore by a self-image that he'd acquired when he was little.

---

83. From Chapter 4 (and the Appendix) you can see how this is an example of Working the Triad in order to achieve synergy. In this case the weak link or missing movement is Lion. Integrating Lion into the interaction would bring about a higher level of relating.

84. And Toto too, but we will cover Toto in the next chapter.

- **We need Scarecrow's awareness.** Scarecrow is objective. He dispassionately observes what is happening and thus is able to introduce new ideas and solutions. As you'll recall, it was Scarecrow who came up with several solutions to navigate the way to Dorothy in the Witch's castle. This led to the inevitable liquefaction of the Witch. When we face our witches, it is crucial to have Scarecrow, the observing side of our mind, come along with us so that we can see our way through the ordeal.

No Shame, No Blame!

There are two common reactions to sensing an inner witch: shame or blame. Shame is that feeling that we are defective – that we are "not OK" – and that we will be seen as such. Where guilt says that we did something bad, shame says that we *are* bad. One of the typical reactions to finding a scary or "bad" aspect in ourselves is to feel disgraced, or to hate or attack ourselves.[85]

The second popular reaction to encountering a witch is to blame someone.[86] Blaming is the process by which we "project" the responsibility for the witch onto something or someone outside of ourselves. This is common among people who are at first confronted with a problem and then react with a "counterattack" by finding fault with the person or group that just confronted them.

With almost three decades of intimately working with people, I can hardly think of a clinical or business client where shame or blame was not the initial reaction to an encounter with an inner witch. Until Scarecrow can help us separate and observe, we generally identify with the witch or project the witch onto the other.[87]

---

85. This is a negative Tin Man (moving – toward) reaction.

86. This is a negative Lion (moving – against) reaction.

87. As previously mentioned, we can also dissociate from the witch as well, which is neither shame nor blame.

This "shame-blame" reaction to a witch is never more prevalent than in an intimate relationship such as marriage. Your partner confronts you about your lack of communication, or perhaps, your disorganization. If what your partner tells you is in fact true and she tells it to you in a non-hostile manner and you still become defensive, more than likely a witch has been aroused.[88] If shame takes over, you cannot look at the situation objectively; instead, you immediately feel bad about yourself.[89] As a result, you might feel overly injured and/or immobilized by the shame, withdraw from your partner, or become defensive or counterattack.[90] None of these reactions, needless to say, help the communication and certainly do not help melt the inner witch.

This is a problem that many organizations face as well. Sometimes leaders do not want to admit that things go wrong, that they have problems, that they make mistakes, or that they need outside help. As one manager once put it, referring to the top executives in the company, "They don't like to hear 'bad news.'" As a result they ignore problems and wish that the witch they do not want to see would just go away. If they do acknowledge the "bad news," they are likely to blame something or someone else for it.

In order to grow, either as individuals, as couples or as an organization, we need to look objectively at what is wrong, without shaming ourselves, becoming defensive or blaming others.

Some transcendent place between shame and blame is the playing field of honest and effective living.

---

88. Being defensive often involves a combination of both shame and blame.

89. This is an example of the myopic nature of witches. They hijack your mind and you are not able to see things from a perspective outside that of the witch.

90. Negative Tin Man (moving-toward), negative Scarecrow (moving-away) and negative Lion (moving-against) respectively.

The Melting Point

As the story draws to its end, we find that Dorothy has benefited from facing the Wicked Witch. It is when she faced what she feared that it melted. And as part of the process, she utilized, realized and strengthened her inner Scarecrow, Tin Man and Lion – capacities of thinking, heart and courage – without the help of any Wizard. All of us become healthier when we face our wicked witches. Such is the case, whether the witch is a truly destructive part of ourselves, a very intense feeling or a phenomenon based on a faulty paradigm. Witches melt when they are confronted.

I worked with a person who had avoided awareness of feeling inferior for most of his life. He would overwork, overcompensate and overreact because of this. He decided to seek help. As he worked through his therapy, he began to let himself become more aware of this inferiority identity. It frightened him that he might actually be what it implied, a loser. In one session, he told me of an experience that he had had that week. He said that he stopped running away and just looked directly at the inferiority feeling – he acknowledged it as something that he was experiencing. He felt the shame but could remain objective in his experiencing of it. As he finished the story, there was a smile of relief on his face, because his sense of being inferior had melted a bit. He beat the witch by confronting her.

As with any witch, if you face up to it and douse it with the living water of truth and grace – awareness without shame – the witch will melt.[91]

Witches don't often melt as completely as Dorothy's witch did in the story, but they do dwindle. Witch-facing is something that we have to

---

91. As you can see, it took all three companions to make this crusade a success. He needed the objectivity and awareness of Scarecrow, the forgiveness or grace of Tin Man and the courage and truth-telling of Lion to confront this formidable witch.

do over and over again. The man who had the encounter with feelings of inferiority still had more feelings of inferiority to face. He will have to face this witch again and again. When he does, she will melt some more. Each time that he faces her it will be easier to face her than the time before, and she will begin to show up less. He will not be as dominated by her, but instead will be freer to live and move through his life.

In psychoanalysis, we talk about the need to "integrate bad objects." This means that when we face and "own" the non-integrated and bad aspects of our "inner world" (in other words, our witches). Whatever you call it, when you face a witch, they melt. They lose their power over us, whether this "bad object" is our rage, dependency, hunger, bad self-image, envy or greed. And when we meet these things head on, over time they get weaker, and eventually, they can integrate and sometimes "disappear" altogether. They melt away. When this happens, we change. Really change!

REFLECTIONS

1. Which witches (pun intended) do you tend to fear the most?

    a.   Moving-against witches of anger and hate

    b.   Moving-toward witches of helpless and weak

    c.   Moving-away witches of aloneness and not belonging

    Please explain.

2. What do you tend to do when you encounter a scary inner witch?

3. Have you ever honestly stopped and faced something that was scary about yourself? What happened as a result?

6. Use Your Resources:

TOTO, MUNCHKINS, GLINDA and the RUBY SLIPPERS

"Won't you go with me?" pleaded the girl, who had begun to look upon the [good witch] as her ... friend.

"No, I cannot do that," she replied; "but I will give you my kiss, and no one will dare injure a person who had been kissed by the Witch of the North."

L. Frank Baum, *The Wonderful Wizard of Oz*

No one can go on our personal journeys for us. The *Wizard of Oz* is primarily a story about personal responsibility. The Wizard did not give Scarecrow a brain, Tin Man a heart nor Lion his courage; rather, they developed each attribute themselves. Likewise, it was up to Dorothy to face and melt her own Wicked Witch and relinquish her fraudulent Wizard. The trip to the Land of Oz was *Dorothy's* journey; it was about *Dorothy's* personal responsibility.

But the *Wizard of Oz* is also a story of dependency and reliance on others. Dorothy could not have successfully completed her journey on her own. From the first Munchkin input to the last advice from Glinda, Dorothy needed and used resources all along the Yellow Brick Road. She could not do it alone.

To be successful in life, especially when we are going through a try-ing time, we have to be both responsible for ourselves *and* reliant on others. This truth is simple and obvious – it is not an *either-or* proposi-tion but rather a *both-and* reality.

It is the wise person who knows when to assume responsibility and when to call for help from others.

When Dorothy first steps onto the Yellow Brick Road, she doesn't know where she is headed. She has never heard of the Emerald City. She sets out alone, without a clear idea of where she is heading or even why she is heading there. Only after she meets and interacts with various friends on whom she can depend is she able to complete her journey along the Yellow Brick Road.

There is a very important lesson in this: We cannot intrinsically change and grow without help from *outside resources*. In real life, as in the story of *The Wizard of Oz*, no one is able to make it down the Yellow Brick Road all alone. It is absurd to presume that we can encounter the unknowns of Oz, face witches, give up our wizards or develop our inner Scarecrow, Tin Man or Lion without outside help. To successfully com-plete life's many journeys, we must depend on others.

In this day and age of "self-reliance," the concept of "depending on someone" often has a negative connotation. In some cases, dependency is in fact unhealthy. In other situations, however, it is anything but weak or wrong. So, it's important to determine the difference between the unhealthy, destructive dependencies – like those on a fraudulent wizard – and the posi-tive ones that are essential for successful and effective living.

Healthy vs. unhealthy dependencies

There are few psychological issues that are more confusing than depen-dency. That's because people are all too often dependent in unhealthy ways, but they shun the more appropriate, beneficial reliance on others. For example, some people regard certain destructive dependencies such as drinking or smoking as "cool." Yet, being able to cry on a confidant's shoulder or seek input from a co-worker is considered a weakness. I can't tell you how often I see clients who want me to tell them what to do with their life but are extremely reluctant when it comes to sharing their sadness.

By now, this might have a familiar ring, reminiscent of the wizards we previously discussed in Chapter Three. Wizards represent unhealthy dependencies in our life – those things or people we seek to magically rescue us instead of relying on our own personal resources.

Although some dependencies keep us immature, not all of them are destructive. In fact, we simply cannot go through a trying time – yet alone grow – without depending on others in some way. Our constant challenge is to discern which dependencies are immature and stifling and which are necessary and healthy. Like so many other things, this ability to discern comes with experience, trial and error and, yes, through the help of others. Here are a couple of keys to keep in mind.

First key: do it yourself

Generally speaking, if you *can* do it yourself, then you probably *should* do it yourself. A toddler can't tie his own shoe, but a teenager is more than able to do so. A teenager asking for help tying his shoe is a sign of something not quite right. Did you know that if you help a baby chick break out of its shell, you will end up imposing a handicap on the chick that could even result in its death? It is the very struggle of breaking the shell that makes the chick strong enough to survive in the outer world. As for Dorothy, she and her three companions obtain brains, a heart and courage, not from the Wizard but from their own struggles and learning.

Doing it yourself has a twist to it. There are some things that we cannot do for ourselves, regardless of our competence. For example: My back is sore, but I cannot possibly give myself a full back massage. I can hardly reach the muscles in my own back much less rub it effectively. To fully massage my back, I need help from someone or something other than myself. This represents the dependency based on things that I simply cannot do for myself. No matter what, there are those things that we cannot do for ourselves. A grammar school athlete cannot drive the car to baseball practice; a client cannot provide his own therapy; a business owner cannot run an entire company on his own.

There is another type of "massage" I'll reference, the *foot rub*. I *can* give myself a foot rub, but no matter what anyone says, a foot rub is better when a capable masseuse does it for you. This analogy illustrates how there are things we are certainly capable of doing for ourselves but it is preferable to ask others to do it.

A child is capable of riding his bike to baseball practice, but it is faster and safer to have a parent drive him. Self-help books can offer assistance to people struggling with emotional issues, but it is not like going through the intensive process of therapy with a trained psychologist. A CEO is capable of typing an address on an envelope, but it would not be the best use of her time. She wisely delegates these tasks to her staff, freeing up her time for executive responsibilities.

Getting perspective on a problem is an example of the "foot rub" dependency. Since our own perspective is inherently limited and biased, it is helpful to seek out someone else's perspective to broaden our view. It does not necessarily mean that their perspective is better or right but it challenges us to think in a different way about a problem to be solved. I often tell my student in graduate school classes that some of my most effective psychological interpretations were wrong, BUT it got the client to think about their situation in a new way.

Take the analogy of several blind people who are standing around an elephant trying to come up with a concept of "an elephant." The one who is standing next to the elephant's hind leg concludes that an elephant is like a tree trunk. Another, who can feel only the elephant's trunk, imagines the elephant as a large snake. Obviously, everyone around the elephant needs help from the others in order to put together a truer picture of what an elephant really looks like. This is why organizations often hire consultants – outside experts – who bring a fresh new perspective to the company.[92]

---

92. People often ask me what I think the flying monkeys represent. If they are familiar with Baum's book they will understand when I suggest that flying

Second key: a positive outcome

The second key to discerning healthy from unhealthy dependency concerns the outcome of a dependency: Healthy dependency in the long run will make us stronger, while unhealthy dependency, eventually if not immediately, weakens us. It is that simple.

Our reliance on a wizard diminishes us, although it may not look that way at first. Someone who turns to alcohol to treat the anxiety might feel better at first. However, in time, this person will likely become more stressed, more depressed and less confident. On the other hand, if the same anxious person calls on a good friend, seeks professional help or prays and meditates, the personality should strengthen.

People often make the criticism that those who are undergoing therapy will become dependent on their therapist. The point is that they will and should become dependent.

The important question is not whether a person will become dependent but rather, is the dependency healthy or not.

If the person in the long run becomes stronger, more confident (positive Lion), can enjoy intimacy with significant others in their life (positive Tin Man) and can think on their own (positive Scarecrow), then the dependency, no matter how intense, is good. On the other hand, if the person grows less confident (negative Tin Man), develops more hostility and resentment (negative Lion) and becomes more detached and isolated (negative Scarecrow), then their dependency on the therapist is

monkeys represent *outside consultants* – people we temporarily hire to help us with a specific problem or need. In the book, whoever was in possession of the *magic cap* could call on the flying monkeys three times to do them a favor. When we first encounter the flying monkeys it is the Wicked Witch of the West who has the cap. She calls on the monkeys to incapacitate the Scarecrow and Tin Man and to deliver Dorothy, Toto and Lion to her. Later in the story, Dorothy obtains the cap and it is her prerogative to use the cap three times to call on the monkeys to help her – as she did.

unhealthy and immature.[93] This example of dependency on a therapist is true for just about any other type of dependency as well.[94]

Dorothy's Four Resources

Dorothy has at least four resources on which she depends during her journey on the Yellow Brick Road. These resources are dependable and necessary. They do things for her that she cannot do for herself. They enrich her experience and make her a stronger person.

For the remainder of this chapter I will concentrate on the four "resources" that Dorothy relied on to get her through her journey: Toto, the Munchkins, Glinda the Good Witch of the North and the Ruby Slippers.

Toto

Dorothy's life became very sad as she grew to understand that it would be harder than ever to get back to Kansas and Aunt Em again.[95] Sometimes she would cry bitterly for hours, with Toto sitting at her feet and looking into her face, whining dismally to show how sorry he was for his little mistress. Toto did not really care whether he was in Kansas or the Land of

---

93. When this unhealthy dependency occurs in therapy, it is almost always with the cooperation of an immature therapist. Immature therapists "rely" on their clients to depend on them in order to make themselves feel important.

94. Including a twelve-step sponsor, spouse, friend, business coach, spiritual mentor, medical advisor, adult child on a parent, etc.

95. In Baum's book, *The Wonderful Wizard of Oz* (from which this excerpt is taken), Dorothy is enslaved and trapped in the Witch's house for an extended time with Toto and Lion. Tin Man and Scarecrow were disabled by the Winged Monkeys and left for dead in the forest. You can see in this excerpt how much Toto – like most dogs – exemplifies moving-toward behaviors and attitudes.

Oz so long as Dorothy was with him; but he knew the little girl
was unhappy, and that made him unhappy too.

Toto, Dorothy's dog, is a constant companion and best friend. Toto
accompanies Dorothy from Kansas to Oz and back again. We all need
a loyal friend like little Toto in our life, especially when we are in the
throes of an Oz experience.

As much as Scarecrow, Tin Man and Lion represent our internal
companions or capacities, I like to think of Toto as an external, or real-
life, companion or comrade. In our experience, this might be a spouse,
a friend, a family member or even a pet – just like Toto. In the work
world, it could be a colleague, classmate, business partner or someone
in the work team. What is essential about our Toto resources is that they
are peers who are loyal and consistently represent a positive influence
in our life.

The Greeks had several words that can be loosely translated to
our word "love." The Greek word *phileo* (pronounced fil-eh'-o), for
instance, means to treat someone affectionately or kindly … to welcome, or befriend. It is a term that refers to a non-erotic, friendship-type
of love and affection. *Phileo* forms the root for the name Philadelphia,
the City of Brotherly Love. Toto represents *phileo* love and concern.

I know someone whose wife had a very serious, near-death accident
several years ago. He tells the story of how his friend from high school,
upon hearing about this, stopped what he was doing, jumped in an airplane and flew across the country to be with him. He was so moved by
this friend's *phileo* love for him that he still cannot tell this story without
a tear coming to his eye. This is the type of friend represented by Toto.

For the most part, our journey down the Yellow Brick Road is an
individual quest. It can be a lonely road. It is helpful, if not necessary, to
have a Toto come along on the journey – *someone who will just be there*
for us. Someone we can talk to, who will listen and care. Toto friends
are not wizards. They do not have magical cures or quick fixes. They
don't make everything better or make bad experiences go away. Toto-
companions just stay by our side and go the distance with us.

A woman lost her teenage son to a strange and sudden illness. Many in her church congregation approached her with empty religious platitudes: "It was God's will," or "She is in a better place now." An acquaintance of mine, instead went to visit with her, brought a few meals, spent the day with her, cried with her and held her hand. He got down into the trenches of life with her. He had no magical cures. He had no advice. He was only a friend who cared; he was a Toto.

In the *Book of Job*, many horrible things afflicted the protagonist in the story. Job lost all he owned and he lost everyone he loved. So-called "friends" came to his aid by telling him what to do and tried to explain why it happened. Later in the story, another friend visits Job. This friend does not say a word of advice but merely sits next to Job and grieves with him. At the end of the book, God rebukes his first group of "friends" but commends Job's last friend. His last friend was a Toto.

Munchkins

Now let's examine the little people Dorothy first encounters on her journey through the Land of Oz: the Munchkins. The Munchkins welcome Dorothy and orient her to the strange land they call Oz. They applaud her for killing someone – explaining that she was a wicked witch who had enslaved them all. They encourage her as she leaves to go to the Emerald City. To me, the Munchkins represent our social community. There is a popular idea that many parents know intuitively:

It takes a village to raise a child. The Munchkins symbolize the village.

We are social creatures, and we live and function in social groups. Throughout recorded history, humans have lived in tribes, clans or communities. The community formulates and maintains our worldview and establishes values and the rules of engagement. We are all part of families, schools, companies, professional organizations, clubs, political parties and a wide variety of social groups.

Social groups provide several functions, of which I will list only a few.

- **Belonging and identity:** Whether you are member of a church or a member of an inner-city gang, the community provides a place where you belong. Inclusion in a group means that you are part of something that is bigger than yourself and whose identity becomes a part of your identity. Belonging is a basic and vital psychological need, and membership in a social group helps meet that need.

- **Guidance and orientation:** Groups teach values. They teach us what to believe and what not to believe. They orient us to the world around us.

- **Support and encouragement:** Once values are instilled, the group supports those values among its members.

- **Rewards and punishment:** Groups provide important feedback. After groups establish values and demonstrate support for them, they then reward or punish accordingly.

- **Protection from "the enemy":** Groups protect the "us" from the "them," whether "them" is a real enemy or just an individual or group that differs from us (such as is the case with business competitors, religious groups or political parties).

Dorothy enters Oz without a map. She is in total awe of her surroundings, but confused. Then come the Munchkins, who help orient Dorothy and give perspective to the very bewildered girl. They provide guidance in a very confusing setting. They even explain how good it is that she has killed someone. They validate her fear of the ugly woman with the pointed hat and her attraction to the beautiful lady in the pretty dress.

They then make clear the route she is to take: the Yellow Brick Road. They applaud her for what she did and encourage her for what she needs to do. They undoubtedly would have done their best to protect her from her enemies.

When we go through an Oz experience, it helps to have a community's support. Whether we are restructuring our company, getting married, grieving the loss of a loved one, or parenting young children, we are helped by the feedback, education, encouragement, correction and protection provided by a community.

For almost two decades I have been a member of a men's group. We are committed to meet on a regular basis, making ourselves available to each other for help, support and guidance. We talk about our lives with our partners, our children, our work and God. We have been there for each other through weddings, divorces, births, death, sickness, sadness and joy. It is not a paid therapy group, just a bunch of men who know that they cannot do the Yellow Brick Road alone.

Let's look at another Munchkin community. Marvin had a problem with sexual addiction. He liked to frequent gay bathhouses, where he would have anonymous sexual experiences. He realized that this was a physically dangerous and psychologically unhealthy behavior. He sought therapy. However, as often is the case with addictions, the individual therapy was not enough. He needed some Munchkins. Because of this, Marvin regularly attended a twelve-step program for his addiction. In this group, he felt he belonged. It educated him on the nature of the addiction and the value of remaining "sober." People were available to him 24-7.[96] And when Marvin reached his one-year-of-sobriety birthday, he was even given special recognition. Marvin's twelve-step program was not perfect. But it was, without a doubt, a "good-enough" community for his journey on the Yellow Brick Road.

---

96. 24 hours a day, seven days a week

Glinda, the good witch

In the movie version of *The Wizard of Oz*, Glinda is the beautiful Good Witch of the North, who every-so-often appears to give Dorothy advice and help.[97] To me, Glinda represents our mentors. She is a sage who is there on occasion and functions more as a *trusted advisor* than as a peer. Though she is friendly, she is not a friend like Toto. She might be part of the community, but she is not the community, *per se*. Glinda is a tutor, an advisor and a mentor to Dorothy as she travels the Yellow Brick Road.

In ancient times "good witches" were wise women or priestesses who were thought to have high powers of healing or wisdom. Who are our *good witches* today? The following are some roles in our society that function for others as a good witch or mentor:

- Parent
- Teacher
- Coach
- Clergy
- Twelve-step sponsor
- Business coach
- Medical doctor
- Expert in given field
- Psychotherapist

It is very important to distinguish good witches from wizards. I realized this when once I was asked during a workshop if I considered myself a wizard. My answer was clear: "Absolutely not! Although a client can make me into a wizard, my role is not that of a wizard. However, I do believe that I am a *good witch* in several of the roles that I play in people's lives – as a psychologist, an organizational consultant, teacher and, most importantly, as a father."

Essentially, the difference between good witches and wizards is the same as the difference between healthy and unhealthy dependencies. As a thera-

---

97. In the book version of the *Wizard of Oz* there were two good witches. The script-writers of the 1939 movie combined the two good witches in to one, Glinda.

pist, I help guide people through an intensive process of growth.[98] As a consultant and lecturer, I help business and community leaders develop interpersonal skills so that they can be more effective in their work. And, as a father, I am available to give love, protection and guidance. In all these roles, I function in a way that is meant to give something to people that they cannot readily give to themselves. In a temporary and limited way I give them something that will hopefully make them stronger and better people. That is what "good witches" and mentors do.

Just as we need a good friend and supportive community, we all at some time in our life need a mentor or a role model, someone who has the maturity or expertise that is needed when we get stuck somewhere along the Yellow Brick Road.

Glinda is by no means the first nor the last literary figure to represent a person who is available to help the hero accomplish his or her mission. Tiresias, the blind prophet of Thebes and the most famous soothsayer of ancient Greece, was just that person. In Greek mythology, Tiresias was a hermaphrodite – half woman, half man – who was available to several Greek mythological heroes on their journey, including Hercules and Odysseus. (Tiresias tried to warn Oedipus of his fate as well, but not everyone listens.) Just as Glinda was available to Dorothy, Tiresias was available for guidance to these men who were on their hero's journey; and s/he provided correction when they went off course. We all need such a person while on our journey through the Land of Oz.

However, many people have difficulty asking others for help. To seek help from someone wiser or more experienced is seen as admitting a weakness or inferiority. Nothing could be further from the truth. The strongest leaders that I know are constantly seeking input from others. They listen to ideas from other people – Totos, Munchkins or Good Witches – and are willing to invest time and money to get input from experts and con-

---

98. I am available for support and acceptance (positive Tin Man), for blunt honesty and good boundaries (positive Lion) and for knowing and observing things about my clients that they cannot – or will not – see (positive Scarecrow).

sultants. They surround themselves with "counselors."[99] This is never more important than when we going through a major life crisis. If you are going through a divorce, someone important to you died, things at work are challenging, more than ever you need to humble yourself and ask for help from a Glinda – a good enough Glinda, that is.

The Good, the Bad and the Ugly

We've looked at three types of resources that can be positive, even necessary, for growth, change and success when we are in the throes of an Oz experience. But obviously, not all resources are the same. In fact some are unhealthy and even detrimental to us. One of the keys to successful living is to know which resources to rely on for help. In this regard …

> … *we are ultimately responsible for the Toto companions, Munchkin groups and the Glinda mentors that we choose.*

We are responsible for the resources that we pick.

When I work with people in intensive psychotherapy, I am always fascinated by the way they naturally begin to change their circle of friendships, associations and mentors. As they begin to change from within, they fluently gravitate toward better Toto comrades, Munchkin communities and Glinda mentors and models. Likewise, as they pick better Toto friends, Munchkin groups and Glinda gurus, they are subsequently helped to change and grow. So which comes first: the changes or the choice of resources? The answer is either! It doesn't matter. Change is dynamic; it happens in both directions.

David Winnicott, a psychoanalyst from England, coined a term that has come to mean a great deal to psychological community. When dis-

---

99. An ancient and enduring tradition.

cussing parents, he noted that there are no ideal or perfect parents. He said that what is important is that they be "good enough."

There is no community, companion or mentor that is perfect. The aim is to find someone who is simply *good enough*. But how does one know if their companion, therapist or support group is *good enough*? To address this question, I will once again use Dorothy's three companions, Scarecrow, Tin Man and Lion. To illustrate this, I will talk about mentors. (However, the principles can be applied to communities and companions as well.) A *good enough* mentor is mature. To be mature one needs the three companions to be integrated into one's life, working together in synergy.[100] Let us look at an example of a mature mentor.

I had a client who was near the end of her therapy and had made many positive changes in her life – including changes in her career. At that time, she had just switched jobs, and she shared something with me regarding her new boss. She mentioned that he was a great listener; he supports her, respects her opinions and can be very honest and direct. He was stable and even-keel in his disposition toward my client.[101] He was quite the opposite of her former boss, who seldom listened to her ideas, constantly miscommunicated, had emotional outbursts and took things in an overly sensitive and personal manner. Her new boss is obviously more integrated and mature. In this case, her personal growth led her to a better Glinda. As a result, this better Glinda-boss will help her become more successful in her career.

I frequently am invited to give lectures on how to select a therapist. The lectures could just as easily be about how to select a mate, community, confidant, supervisor, sponsor, etc. As I speak, I use the following chart that compares what I call an "impaired therapist" to a "good enough" therapist.

---

100. Please see Chapter 4 and Appendix II for information on the three companions and synergy.

101. Positive Tin Man, Lion and Scarecrow, respectively.

Table 1. The "Impaired Therapist" vs. the "Good Enough" Therapist

"Impaired" Therapist Move-Toward (Negative) Tin Man	"Good Enough" Therapist Move-Toward (Positive) Tin Man
• Keeps poor boundaries with client • Overly influenced by client • Would rather be a "buddy" than professional • Tries to do more than is realistic • Fears or avoids confrontation • Needs to be liked by client	• Empathic, tuned in to client, good listener • Respect, positive regard for client • Can focus attention on client • Capacity for emotional connection • Things are done for the client's best interest
OR **Move-Against (Negative)** **Lion**	*AND* **Move-Against (Positive)** **Lion**
• Overly controlling, takes charge • Blames the client • Impatient, rushed, shaming, judgmental, guilt-inducing • Hostile (overt or covert) • Strongly needs to be admired	• Maintains good boundaries • Sets and keeps limits • Not afraid to confront client • Willing to tell the truth, be honest • Has self-regard and self-protection, self-confidenc
OR **Move-Away (Negative)** **Scarecrow**	*AND* **Move-Away (Positive)** **Scarecrow**
• Detached, has hard time connecting, very low involvement, indifferent, passive • Avoids difficult emotions, "heady," does not want to be affected • Distant, preoccupied	• Professional, neutral, unbiased, objective • Paced, not rushed • Leaves plenty of room for the client • Contains their own feelings, non-reactive

As you can see, on the left side of the chart there are three types of *impaired* helpers. If you have a therapist who consistently acts like any of these three, consider getting a new therapist. If you have a mate like any of these, I suggest counseling. If you have a supervisor like any of these … good luck!

On the right side of the table are the attributes of a *good-enough* helper. As you can see, it is the combination of all three movements working together that makes a healthy and integrated helper. If you have a therapist like this, go full speed ahead in your therapy. If you have a mate like this, nurture and treasure him or her. If you have a supervisor like this, consider yourself fortunate.

Although the above table describes a particular type of Glinda-therapist, it also applies to any Glinda-mentors, Toto-companions and Munchkin-communities. Remember that *we are personally responsible for choosing our resources*. At the risk of sounding corny: Birds of a feather flock together, and if your flock is going in the wrong direction, change flocks!

If we are traveling on the Yellow Brick Road through a challenging Oz experience, we cannot survive without help from dependable people and responsible organizations. We are social creatures. We need to be interpersonally connected, enriched, taught, challenged and encouraged. Our need for this input and help is never so important as when we are thrown in to the Land of Oz by a significant life twister. I can't imagine the outcome if Dorothy had not had help from Glinda, the Munchkins and Toto. Neither can I imagine how I could make it on my own personal life journey without the help of my companions, community and trusted advisors. We need each other if we dare to travel the Yellow Brick Road.

Ruby Slippers

The leader of the winged monkeys flew up to her, his long, hairy arms stretched out and his ugly face grinning terribly; but he saw the mark of the Good Witch's kiss upon her forehead and stopped short, motioning the others not to touch her.

"We dare not harm this little girl," he said to them, "for she is protected by the Power of Good, and that is greater than the Power of Evil.... The Wicked Witch was both surprised and worried when she saw the mark on Dorothy's forehead, for she knew well that neither the Winged Monkeys nor she, herself, dare hurt the girl in any way.[102]

We come to one last resource, which is different from the others. The resources thus far are strictly interpersonal in nature. This fourth resource involves personal faith. I realize that this last "resource" will not appeal to everyone. However, for many people their personal faith is truly something that they rely on to get them through many of their visits to the Land of Oz.

Glinda gives Dorothy a pair of ruby slippers to wear on her journey and warns her: "Never let those ruby slippers off your feet for a moment or you will be at the mercy of the Wicked Witch of the West." In the book version, Dorothy is given instead a kiss from the Good Witch. In the book, it is the kiss that protects her from harm. "I will give you my kiss, and no one will dare injure a person who has been kissed by the Witch of the North," she says.

The slippers and the kiss both represent the same thing: ultimate good or protection. It is the faith in the Ultimate Good that will see you through most anything. An essential part of any form of spirituality is faith, since spirituality by definition involves matters neither seen nor measured. For many people, faith is an important resource with which to travel the Yellow Brick Road. Instead of advocating a particular religious practice or belief system, I am suggesting faith itself.[103] Sometimes the faith is not even a belief in a deity *per se,* but faith still in an Ultimate Good out their in the universe.

---

102. Baum, *op. cit.*

103. Although I come from and adhere to a Judeo-Christian "faith," I acknowledge the powerful dynamic of faith in something outside of oneself (or an Ultimate Good) that is common in most forms of spirituality.

When acrobats perform a high-wire act, there is a safety net below the wire to catch them if they fall. Faith is the ultimate safety net. Dorothy has the Slippers or the Kiss to ultimately "catch" her if something is to threaten her. Those who have faith believe that Something or Someone bigger than them, an "Ultimate Good," will catch them. All through history, human beings have had faith, in this sense. Some might say that this is merely a psychological fabrication to help us cope. Even if this were the case, this so-called fabrication appears to help many people.

This type of faith is not necessarily magical thinking, where God is the Supreme Bellhop, ready to give us room service for every whim and wish. Nor is this faith a magical guarantee that you will never be harmed. In other words, Ultimate Good is not necessarily a wizard.

We want wizards to make things easy and fix things fast. Healthy faith is not like that; it helps people endure through suffering, not avoid it.

Belief in an Ultimate Good does not counter reality – it helps us deal with reality and occasionally transcend it.

This belief in an Ultimate Good has helped many people through the most difficult adventures on the Yellow Brick Road, including broken relationships, death of a loved one, financial difficulties and various personal failures. Personal faith has helped them move forward into the Haunted Forest to face the Wicked Witch. It has provided the Presence that holds them when they are in an uncharted Oz experience. It sustains when one renounces a personal wizard without having an immediate replacement. A person's faith can give context to the complex process of integrating Scarecrow, Tin Man or Lion into their life.

A Conclusive Example

I will conclude with the example of a well-known organization, the twelve-step program. The twelve-step programs have been remarkably successful in helping addicts recover from tenacious addictions where other programs fail. It should be no surprise that these programs have naturally coordinated all the components of the resources mentioned in this chapter.

People in twelve-step programs are part of a community. They are a bunch of *Munchkins* who meet for the purpose of helping each other stay clean and sober. They teach and interpret the twelve steps, the rules and guidelines of the organization to help people get and stay sober.

Although they function as a group, they also are available to each other as *Toto-friends*. They do this as understanding peers and without judgment. I know someone who recently went to a twelve-step program for the first time. Of the sixteen people attending the meeting that night, at least six of them gave him their phone numbers and told him to call them any time, day or night.

A vital aspect of the twelve-step program involves working with a sponsor, a person within the program who has achieved a recognized level of sobriety and maturity. A sponsor takes on the role of *Glinda* by serving as a mentor to a person who is still working on his or her sobriety.

Finally, one of the key components of the twelve-step philosophy is that of belief in a "Higher Power." It is a faith in Someone or Something that is bigger than oneself, a resource for an addict in his powerlessness to deal with his addiction.

In this one organization, we find all the resources that Dorothy finds in her journey.

In order to travel successfully along the Yellow Brick Road, we need to depend on outside resources and helpers. When we are going through a difficult time and want to grow through the experience rather than succumb to it, we need the help of people and things outside of ourselves. This is not a sign of weakness, nor is it the unhealthy reliance on wizards. It is necessary for success. No one need feel guilty for the help they receive. There will come many times when you will be repaying the favor to someone else who is trying to find their way back home from the Land of Oz via the Yellow Brick Road!

REFLECTIONS

1. Please identify someone or some group that fills each of these resources in your life currently:	2. How would you rate each of these people/groups on a scale of health, with 7 being Very Healthy and 1 being Not Healthy at All?
Toto: _____	1 2 3 4 5 7
Glinda: _____	1 2 3 4 5 7
Munchkins: _____	1 2 3 4 5 7

3. Think of a crisis that you have gone through in your life. What people and groups/organizations were there for you?

4. Are you a Toto or a Glinda for anyone in your life at this time? Do you belong to any groups that function as Munchkins for its members?

5. How would you describe your spirituality? Do your spiritual beliefs of faith provide a support for your visits into the Land of Oz?

7. There's No Place Like Home

Is Change Really Possible?

"You are certainly as good as you are beautiful! But you have not yet told me how to get back to Kansas" [declared Dorothy].

"Your silver shoes will carry you over the desert," replied Glinda. *"If you had known their power you could have gone back to your Aunt Em the very first day you came to this country."*

"But then I should not have had my wonderful brains!" cried the Scarecrow. *"I might have passed my whole life in the farmer's cornfield."*

"And I should not have had my lovely heart," said the Tin Woodman. *"I might have stood and rusted in the forest till the end of the world."*

"And I should have lived a coward forever," declared the Lion, *"and no beast in all the forest would have had a good word to say to me."*[104]

---

104. Baum, *op. cit.*

Dorothy returned to Kansas a new person. Through her experience on the Yellow Brick Road, she developed and matured her Tin Man heart, her Lion courage and her Scarecrow knowing. She faced and melted a scary witch. She unmasked a fraudulent wizard. She learned how to use the healthy resources availed to her. By taking the hero's journey, Dorothy grew up. Dorothy changed.

"It is easy to have a fictional character in a story experience true change. But what about me" you might ask. Are we truly able to change?

The Road Less Traveled

Change is difficult. Because of this, not everyone wants to change. Enduring change is an unsettling and often painful experience. It means going from the known to the unknown. For some people, change is too painful to bear. Others simply don't want to change. It's not that their lives are fine just as they are; these individuals consciously or unconsciously fear change. Still others believe they are incapable of changing.

Is change really possible?

Creating genuine, long-lasting change sometimes seems unlikely, especially as we get older. With each passing year, it seems as though we become more entrenched in old habits. Certainly we can learn new skills, such as how to use a computer or play golf. As adults, we continue to acquire volumes of information from a variety of sources: reading, television, conversations, seminars, etc. This is not what people are talking about, however, when they ask about the possibility of real change. They want to know if their reactions to emotionally charged situations can be altered; whether they can significantly alter how they think about themselves; if it's possible to modify their responses to others at work or at home.[105]

---

105. The type of change that I am suggesting here is related to the common idea of "emotional intelligence" made popular by the work of Daniel Goleman.

When people ask about change, what they really want to know is if they can change "intrinsically." The word intrinsic implies the inherent and essential nature of something. When we say something in us is intrinsic, we mean that it is a basic part of us. It pertains to something that is genuinely internalized – a part of our repertoire. It is reflexive and automatic. By the time we reach adulthood, brushing our teeth or driving a car are intrinsic parts of our life. I do not have to relearn how to brush my teeth every night. In fact, it is so intrinsic I can do other things such as walk around, watch television, read a letter or surf the Internet while I am brushing my teeth. Intrinsic change is change that has become a basic part of us.

"Extrinsic," on the other hand, comes from a Latin word meaning external or "from without." Extrinsic pertains to something that is not part of a natural response pattern. Take for example, learning to ski. At first, every attempt to get down the hill is a conscious and forced effort. We have to talk ourselves through every little move that the ski instructor demonstrated. However, after much persistence – and a lot of falling down – our mind and body starts to learn this complex physical task. Eventually one is able to downhill ski with a natural ease. Learning to ski has gone from an extrinsic experience to an intrinsic one. We can eventually ski without thinking about it.

For young children, learning is mostly intrinsic. They are like little "learning organisms." Since they have so little to unlearn and because their minds are developmentally "ready," much of what they learn immediately becomes part of them. For instance, a child learning her first words does so almost by osmosis: "Mommy" and "Daddy" and other words organically enter her vocabulary. Except in the cases of children who experience developmental difficulties, children essentially latch onto speaking quickly. However, when we study a foreign language as adults, we spend hours on end memorizing vocabulary words, trying to put together a sentence that makes sense. It is only after a great extrinsic effort that we become intrinsically fluent in a second language.

The same is true for psychological learning. Our attitudes and behaviors toward others and ourselves are established through very early interactions with significant people in our lives (such as parents, grandparents, nannies, etc.). During these developmentally critical early years a child learns things like who they are, how to respond to emotionally charged events and how to treat and relate to others.[106]

The good part about intrinsic change is that once you learn behaviors, you do not have to *relearn* them. You can go on with your routines without concentrating on your every move. They become *habit*. These habits also include how we perceive ourselves and the attitudes we have toward ourselves, the opposite sex, authority, people who are not like us, and moods that we carry around internally.[107]

The unfortunate part about intrinsic change is that once you learn behaviors, they are hard to change. Sometimes these learned behaviors are negative habits, attitudes and perceptions. It is these negative habits that cripple us at work and at home. People who *can* change their negative personal and interpersonal habits are more adaptive to life and as a result are more happy and fulfilled. On the other hand, people who are unable to change their "dysfunctional" personal and interpersonal patterns are destined to be less adaptive and therefore less able to live an effective and therefore happier life.

In conclusion, I do believe that change is possible … but not easy. But living a life dominated by unhealthy and unhappy habits of thinking, feeling and behaving is no less difficult than changing, and is ultimately more painful. The difficult road of change is, as Robert Frost suggests, the road less traveled. The hero's journey to healthy intrinsic change is

---

106. Our personality is based on the dynamic interaction of three ingredients: genetics, experience and choice. The first, genetics, involves the traits that we inherit from our biological parents such as the color of our eyes, our temperament, biochemical proclivities, etc. The second is what we are referring to here, our early life and formative experience of childhood. The third is what we are addressing in this book, the moral and psychological choices we make as adults.

107. These ingrained attitudes and perceptions are sometimes called "paradigms." Stephen Covey, in his book *The Seven Habits of Highly Effective People*, describes paradigms as our internal "maps" or models of ourselves and the world in which we live.

daunting, but invaluable if taken. For those of you who dare to travel this road, I wish you all the best and Godspeed on the Yellow Brick Road.

Afterword

I trust that this small book has given you some guidance and inspiration. L. Frank Baum's wonderful story of Dorothy and her trip to the Land of Oz. provided a wonderful format for me to communicate these principles that I hold so dearly and have found so helpful for myself as well as for those I've worked with over the last three decades.

I strongly encourage the reader, if you are at all interested in the Interpersonal Triad, to continue reading Appendix I.

Please contact the author via the website below if you are interested in taking the *Interpersonal Triad Inventory* or for information regarding materials or workshops based on the principles written about herein for:

- Personal or spiritual growth
- Leadership or organizational development
- Marriage enrichment, communication; or
- Parenting.

Dr. Sam Alibrando, www.yellowbrickroad-book.com.

Appendix I

A Closer Look at

THE THREE COMPANIONS

The Interpersonal Triad – moving away, toward and against – represented so wonderfully by Dorothy's companions, is the centerpiece of
how we effectively interact with others. In this Appendix we will go
deeper into the ideas introduced in Chapter 4. Admittedly it will be more
"academic" than the main body of the book, but I recommend the interested reader to carry on through the psychological language to get to the
prize at the end: how we use the Interpersonal Triad to change.

Here we will look at the four *characteristics* of the Interpersonal
Triad. These characteristics further define the movements and how they
relate to each other. We will then look at four sets of *positive behaviors*
that correspond to the characteristics. These behaviors describe what an
interpersonally effective person would look like. We will conclude with
a discussion of a process called *working the triad* – how people change
using the Interpersonal Triad.

Table 1. The four characteristics and behaviors

	Characteristics of the Movements ...	Positive Behaviors
1	Movements are Either Positive or Negative	Behaviors that are More Positive than Negative
2	Movements Fit a Context	Behaviors that Appropriately Fit Context
3	Movements are Common & Connected	Behaviors that are Flexible
4	Movements are Dynamic	Behaviors that Manifest Synergy

Characteristics of the Three Movements: Movements are Either Positive or Negative.

Each movement or companion can be either positive or negative. The positive effect of any movement results in something that is constructive and creative. It is life-giving and energy-producing. It makes things better. When there is a positive connection there is often clear, and thus successful, communication.

- Harry buys each member in his work group a present that reflects their unique contributions to a project. This is an example of a positive Tin Man (moving-toward). It was a clear and successful communication of his gratitude.

- Mary tells her father to please stop tickling her because it is uncomfortable. This is a positive moving-against communication (Lion).

On the other hand, the negative effect in a movement is destructive instead of constructive. It brings about a depreciated result and uses more energy than it gives. It is anti-life and anti-creative and results in disconnection and poor communication.

- Harry feels guilty for asking his team to work so hard and fears that they will not like him. As a result, he does most of the work himself, even staying at the office during evenings after everyone else leaves. This is an example of enabling, or negative, Tin Man (moving-toward).

- When Mary's father begins to tickle her, she reacts by calling him a "stupid idiot." This is an ineffective moving-against (negative Lion) communication. It sets the father up to react scornfully to her rather than to understand her displeasure at being tickled.

Each movement can be either positive or negative in its effect. In essence we end up with six possibilities – two pairs of three movements; one set of movements that are positive and one set of movements that are negative. The following are some examples of both positive and negative expressions of each movement. I start with a general description of each of the six categories. After these, I give an example from love life – with a partner, and one from work life – as a supervisor.

Moving Toward (Tin Man)

Positive Effect	Negative Effect
Considerate/Caring: • Empathy, put self in other's shoes; feel for other people • Intimacy, closeness, togetherness • Healthy dependency, rely on the other, need other	**Compliant:** • Unhealthy or immature dependency; depends on others' opinions and approval to feel good • Very sensitive to rejection and abandonment • Takes things personally • Feels "less-than" other people
Considerate Partner: • Put partner's needs ahead of own needs • Express affection and appreciation, take time to listen to the concerns of partner • Physical and sensual intimacies, tender • Rely on partner for appropriate needs (e.g., conversation, support, affection, sex, encouragement)	**Compliant Partner:** • Sees partner as responsible for their happiness; victim or martyr mentality • Is overly dependent on partner's opinion and approval • Overreacts to partner's dissimilarity • Manipulative, guilt inducing • Needs a lot of reassurance and security
Considerate Supervisor: • Friendly with and interested in those who work with and for them • Listens carefully to the concerns and ideas of others; respects the const ructive input from everyone; Considers others' feelings • Relies on the opinions and input of others	**Compliant Supervisor:** • Overly concerned with being liked by workers, too lenient • Fears others and sees others as better than themselves • Keeps poor boundaries with workers, too friendly (does not engender respect of workers).

Moving Against (Lion)

Positive Effect	Negative Effect
Courageous:	**Contemptuous:**
• Healthy concern for self	• Sees others as less-than self
• Assertive, appropriately aggressive to pursue one's needs	• Preoccupied with self, self centered
• Able to confront others, stands up for self or one's group	• Hostile, inappropriately aggressive, violent
• Clear, honest, truthful, say what they see	• Blaming, critical, judgmental, "seldom wrong"
	• Wants to be in control, bullying, pushes people around, power hungry
Courageous Partner:	**Contemptuous Partner:**
• Takes active responsibility for their own happiness	• Domineering over partner, controlling, insists on their way most of the time, intimidating
• Confronts partner honestly re. their needs and differences	
• Clear honest communication: As interested in truth as in protecting partner's feelings	• Self-centered, their needs predominate over partner's
• Initiates … sexual experiences, activities, problem solving	• Highly critical of partner's imperfections or failures
Courageous Supervisor:	**Contemptuous Supervisor:**
• Confident and self-assured, assertive	• Impatient, easily loses temper
• Will confront people when necessary	• Overly critical and demanding, discourteous to support staff, back-bites supervisors
• Will state opinion, clearly and without apology	• Disrespects the opinions and feelings of workers
• Not overly concerned about what others think of them	• Authoritarian in a non-authoritarian setting, belligerent
• Strong negotiator	

Moving Away (Scarecrow)

Positive Effect	Negative Effect
Cognizant	**Concealed**
• Reflective, think before acting, objective	• Detached, avoiding, uninvolved
• Don't take things personally, don't get hurt easily	• Cut off from feelings, uses thoughts instead of feeling
• Appropriately sensitive, not over-reactive·	• Avoids closeness and conflict, wants to be left alone, prefers things to people
• Psychologically separate	• Play-acts, role plays, acts "as if"
• Endures, tolerates discomfort	
Cognizant Partner:	**Concealed Partner:**
• Does not take partner's mood or criticisms personally; not over-reactive to partner	• Avoids conflict and avoids intimacy with partner
• Able to tolerate separation from partner	• Lacks interest or attachment to partner, more involved with hobbies or work
• Allows partner to develop their own interests, relationships, etc.	• Does not rely on partner
Cognizant Supervisor:	**Concealed Supervisor:**
• Knowing, rational and aware of what is occurring	• Stays in their office they have to interact with others
• When confronted by worker, they do not automatically take it personally, but are able to evaluate responsibility	• Seldom gives praise or asks about how someone is doing
• Thinks and acts rather than reacts	• Avoids conflict at all costs, very awkward if conflict occurs

Movements Fit a Context

Now let's consider a second characteristic of the movements, the context in which a movement takes place. Allow me to illustrate:

Reggie, almost without warning, went up to John and knocked him flat on his back. This would be a negative moving-against in most cases. However, Reggie happens to be a defensive tackle for a football team who was knocking down an opposing player.

Tony walked into his CFO's office to give her one last project before she was finished for the evening. Instead of putting the project in her in-box, he walked up behind her and touched the back of her neck. Sexual harassment you might ask? No. The CFO is also his wife.

The two examples above illustrate how the context in which a movement takes place is an essential characteristic to consider. At first Dorothy moved away from the Wicked Witch. In most circles, this would be considered wise. However, when it became necessary to apprehend her broom, the context changed. At one moment Dorothy is confronting the nasty Lion who just threatened her best friend, Toto, and at another time she is reassuring him as a friend. The movements exist in a context and the context is vital to understanding the nature of the movement.

Another important aspect of context has to do with how a person behaves in a given context. A particular context can bring out different movements in the same person. For example, Mike, when he is around his critical boss, is typically compliant if not self-effacing (an immobilized Tin Man). However, when he gets around employees, he becomes very faultfinding and inconsiderate (a cowardly Lion). Like Mike, we are not the same in different contexts.

Movements are Common and Connected

A third characteristic has to do with the fact that all three movements are *common* to all people and connected with each other. All three movements are part of being human. As metaphors go, Dorothy *was* Scarecrow, Tin Man and Lion. You and I *are* Scarecrow, Tin Man and

Lion. If we refer to someone as having a moving-against personality, what we are really saying is that she typically acts in a moving-against fashion. We are not saying, however, that she does not have a Tin Man (move-toward) or Scarecrow (move-away) aspect to her personality. We express all three movements in some form or fashion – if not directly, then indirectly; if not in a positive way, then in a negative manner.

Sally was a woman who was one of the sweetest people you would ever meet. You wouldn't think that she had a "moving-against" bone in her body. I was a relatively new therapist when I began to see her and I was about to learn an important lesson. For some reason, she became unhappy with her therapy, but never told me what it was. Instead of directly talking about it with me (a healthy moving-against), she simply quit coming for sessions, never returned my calls, and failed to pay the significant balance on her bill. You see, even the sweetest person in the world has a moving-against side. If it does not surface directly it will come out indirectly (e.g. not paying her bill). For people who are indirect in moving against, it will show up in sickness or accidents, in development of a "victim" identity, in passive aggressive behavior, or in having an aggressive or even abusive partner. Everyone has all three of these movements within him or her.

The Interpersonal Triad is not only common to everyone, but all three movements are connected. We cannot understand one without the other two. Each movement must be considered in conjunction with the other two. We cannot understand aggression (against) without understanding love (toward) or without understanding thinking (away). I find it helpful to illustrate Interpersonal Triad by means of a triangle, as illustrated below.[108]

---

108. In fact, I originally called the model the *Interpersonal Triangle*.

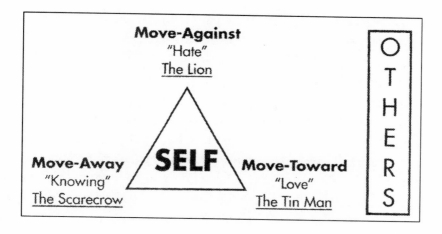

The Interpersonal Triad. The triangle links all three movements together so that all are inter-related. The moving-against is "over and against" the outside world of Others; the moving-toward is "under and toward" the world of Others and the moving-away is away from the world of Others.

Movements are Dynamic

Not only are the movements connected, they also dynamically interact with each other. Each movement will act on the other two for either a positive or a negative effect. Consider this most important dynamic:

> *If for reason of anxiety or habit, we avoid the expression of one movement, we almost always express the negative version of the other movements.*

For example, suppose you are a supervising a difficult employee. He repeatedly turns in poor products, which you have to redo. This is not acceptable and a confrontation is in order. However, if you are afraid of confrontation (moving-against) you might compensate by avoiding this person (negative moving-away) or paradoxically being overly nice to him out of fear of being disliked (negative Tin Man). In this example the fear in one movement – of honest confrontation – negatively effects the other two movements.

The same but opposite dynamic is true with the positive expression of the movements. I referred to this in Chapter 4 as *synergy*. Synergy comes from the Greek word *synergos,* meaning "working together." It is defined as the *integration* of two or more agents so that their combined or cooperative effect is actually *greater than the sum of their individual effects*. In other words, when the three positive movements work together in a coordinated fashion, the quality of each individual movement improves – our caring is deeper, our courage is stronger and our knowing is wiser. AND the overall quality of our interpersonal relationships reaches new levels.

On the surface, the interpersonal movements seem at odds with each other. For example, moving-against (regard for oneself) seems contradictory to moving-toward (regard for others). However, one important quality of synergy is that each movement actually *corrects* the other. When the movements work together, each keeps the other movements from becoming out of balance. For example, when synergy takes place ...

- **Lion** cannot be too mean; he is regulated by Tin Man's regard for others and Scarecrow's self-control and objectivity.

- **Tin Man** is never so weak and helpless because Lion will not give up self-respect and Scarecrow can think on his feet.

- **Scarecrow** will never be so emotionally detached or relationally isolated, because Tin Man's concern for others and Lion's self-interest will not allow Scarecrow to go too far away.

A second quality of synergy is that each interpersonal movement interacts with the others in a way that *augments* the overall effect. The whole is truly greater than the sum of its parts. When our inner Scarecrow, Tin Man and Lion work together, each companion's distinctive strength improves the others and helps us become more whole and effective. Even though these attributes can appear to be contradictory, when they work in concert the result is a really great team![109]

Positive Behaviors

For each characteristic there is a corresponding set of positive behaviors, a measure of interpersonal success and effectiveness. In the following sections we will revisit each characteristic and discuss the positive behaviors related to each characteristic.

Behaviors that are more positive than negative

It almost goes without saying that the best outcome results when all three movements are expressed in the positive.[110] Now a funny thing happens when we express only the positive of each of the three movements: *synergy happens*. Each of the three positive competencies – Considerate Tin Man (moving-toward), Courageous Lion (moving-against) and Cognizant Scarecrow (moving-away) – *cannot* operate by themselves. Interpersonal Synergy happens *only* when each of these three qualities are positively operating *together*. You see ...

- A considerate person (moving-toward) without courage or thinking is merely another nice dependent guy or gal. Without

---

109. Remember the 1980 Olympic amateur U.S. Hockey team.

110. This is so simple that we teach this to children. We tell them to have good manners and to be considerate of others (Positive Tin Man), how and when to express anger and how to compete (Positive Lion), and how to settle down and think before they act (Positive Scarecrow).

self-respect he has no backbone; without objectivity and psychological separation he is overly sensitive and easily affected. Courage and mindfulness make a caring person who is truly a help to others.

- A courageous person (moving-against) who isn't considerate and mindful is merely a self-centered egotist. Without care and regard for others, he is merely a self-serving opportunist; without endurance, self-control and self-awareness, he is also reckless and impetuous with people's dignity and feelings. Caring and consciousness make the courageous person truly powerful.

- A cognizant person (moving-away) without care and courage is merely a detached intellect. Without heart, he is a callous, heartless academic; and without courage he is an overly cautious bore. Courage and caring make the knowing person dynamically wise.

So in essence there is truly only one positive response: a synergistic response with all three positive expressions working together to create a desired effect. Otherwise there are going to be lopsided or out-of-balance behaviors where one or more negative expressions will manifest.

Behaviors that appropriately fit context

A second set of positive behaviors relates to context. How well do we understand and discern the context of our interactions to know which movement is called for at that particular moment? This quality has to do with both how well we *read a situation* and the quality of the chosen reaction or *wisdom*.

How well do we see reality at any moment?

George has a very critical self-image. Because of this, he often perceives his subordinates as being critical when they are, in fact, only trying to communicate their needs, interests and ideas. So when Madeline offers an alternative approach to a problem during a meeting, George takes it as a "put down" and reacts in an aggressive and critical manner (negative Lion). George reads the situation incorrectly and reacts in a hostile manner, when a more reflective (Scarecrow) and more receptive (Tin Man) posture would be appropriate.

In addition to the ability to read the situation accurately, one must still decide how to react. This is the place for *wisdom*. Wisdom knows what to do and when to do it. Wisdom improvises without notes. It is the ability to do the "right" thing in a particular context. For example, is it ever proper to hit someone? The answer is yes, if you are a professional boxer or someone is trying to abduct your child. In most cases hitting someone would be a negative expression of Lion, but there are times when it would be a courageous Lion expression. The difference is all in the context, and wisdom knows the difference.

A woman makes tender, if not sexual, advances toward her partner. In most contexts, the typical response would be to reciprocate with a tender or sexual response (moving-toward). We would question the *wisdom* of his response, however, if her partner criticizes her for her appearance (negative Lion) or escapes into the office to "go online" (negative Scarecrow).

Behaviors that are flexible

A third set of positive behaviors, related to the third characteristic, has to do with flexibility. All three movements are part of being human, however, no one executes all three with the same capacity. All of us are born with temperaments that predispose us to certain strengths and weaknesses. And even if we were born with a potentially perfect balance among the three movements, we would soon lose this balance if our early family experience pressured us to be a certain way in the family.

Simply stated, the more flexible we are in the positive expressions of the movements, the better our relationships. Negatively stated, if a person is stiff, awkward or afraid of one movement, the more out of balance and negative their relationships will be. People who are more limber are better able to move equally and easily between the movements and thus function better in the world. They function better because they adapt to what is needed at any particular moment in any particular situation.

I have found over the years, in working with the Interpersonal Triad model that the key is not to focus on the negative behaviors that we are doing but to pay attention to the *positive behavior that we are NOT doing*. I call the movement that is NOT being expressed the *Missing Movement*.[111]

The Missing Movement is avoided because of the fear and anxiety connected to it.[112] And as we stated earlier, when we under-use one movement we will most likely use the remaining movement(s) in a lop-sided negative manner.

Let me illustrate this with the example of a woman whom I coached. Margaret was the manager of a sales department. She was very afraid of being vulnerable and dependent (she was not flexible when it came to her Tin Man, or moving toward). As a result she liked to be in control at all times, a quality that rendered her domineering and critical of others (negative Lion). She was afraid to move towards, so she moved against. When being controlling and critical did not work for her, she tended to withdraw and emotionally disconnect from people (Negative Scarecrow). Margaret's missing movement was moving-toward. She had the most difficulty being vulnerable and respecting other people. She had a hard time listening to and communicating with people who reported to her. Margaret did not have balanced capacity or flexibility. She was like a tripod with one short leg. This behavioral rigidity clearly handicapped her work as a manager.

This pattern of imbalance might be the same for a person in other settings, such as at home, in a marriage. Often, however, these patterns change from situation to situation. For example, Margaret's husband was

---

111. Or the Least Preferred Movement – LPM – in previous editions of the book.

112. A person's least preferred movement or missing movement is related to the "weak link" discussed in Chapter 4. It is the movement they are least likely to use.

a particularly angry and controlling person himself. In this situation, she was afraid to confront him (Lion) and therefore generally avoided him (Negative Scarecrow), resulting in a very detached marriage. But also, because her husband reminded her so much of her overbearing father, she fell into her old childhood pattern of compliance when she did relate to him (negative Tin Man). In this situation, Margaret's missing movement is Courageous Lion. And the absence of Lion's courage keeps her out of balance and negative in her interactions with her husband.

Behaviors that manifest synergy

This leads us to the fourth and perhaps most important quality: *synergy*. Scarecrow, Tin Man and Lion eventually began working as a finely coordinated team. When they had to infiltrate the Wicked Witch's castle to save Dorothy, they had to co-operate. Individually, they were helpless, but as a team they were not to be stopped. With their combined and collaborative efforts, they not only made it into the castle, but also they freed Dorothy to confront and melt the witch. This integration of capacities is called "synergy."

The same is true with our own inner Scarecrow, Tin Man and Lion: when they work together, each companion's quality corrects and augments the others and we become more whole people.

But how does this happen? The answer is to *work the triad.*

Working the Interpersonal Triad

The missing movement is the key to change.

What is crucial for change is NOT what you are doing that is negative, but it is the positive movement that you are not doing!

When you integrate the positive behaviors of the least preferred companion, you activate a synergistic effect leading to change. Not only are you now benefiting from the use of the positive form of this underused movement, but you also improve the quality of the other two. Most importantly, you bring the three movements together as a higher functioning unit or team. In other words, synergy takes place and therefore change takes place.

I call this process *working the triad*. This most important application of the Interpersonal Triad activates synergy. The steps go something like this:

- **Acknowledge** that you are out of balance and exhibiting negative expressions of the movements or companions.

- **Identify** the *missing movement* (by using your lopsidedness).

- **Integrate** the positive expression of the missing movement.

Let's take Dorothy's three companions as an example. As we know, a chain is no stronger than its weakest link. From an early age it was obvious to me that the Cowardly Lion was her weakest link. While lying on the floor as children watching the annual presentation of the *Wizard of Oz* on television, it was always frustrating to watch Lion. Why didn't he get his act together and just be brave?! Using the model of working the triad it is easy to identify Dorothy's *missing movement*. Dorothy's three companions were out of balance – lopsided. Tin Man was frozen with fear and compliant (negative moving-toward) and Scarecrow was avoidant (negative moving-away). Who was missing? Courageous Lion!

It wasn't until they three companions found themselves looking down on the witch's castle where Dorothy was held prisoner that things changed. Scarecrow declared that he had a plan for how to get into the witch's castle and commissioned Lion to lead them. After a moment's hesitation, we could see the shift in Lion's resolve. "All right, I'll go in there for Dorothy. Wicked witch or no wicked witch; guards or no guards, I'll tear 'em apart." Lion let out a muffled roar, "roof, roof," and then continued, "I may not come out alive but I'm going in there."

It was when the cowardly lion became courageous – outside the witch's castle – that things changed. When Lion found his nerve, the team found synergy. When Lion courageously committed, Scarecrow thought of a way into the castle and Tin Man moved with passion and heart. Later in the story the same thing happened with the Wizard. With Lion's newfound courage, they all confronted the Wizard when he refused their wishes, even after they had produced the broom that he'd requested. As a result of this synergistic interaction (with a little help from a friend, Toto) they exposed the Wizard's true character – he was a humbug fraud.

The missing movement for Margaret in the example above (at work) was not Lion but Tin Man. And because of that she was out of balance in relation to those she supervised. As you will remember, she was controlling (negative moving against) and distant (negative moving away). What was missing? Tin Man! Margaret would not only be more flexible if she acquired more Tin Man capacities at work, but the quality of the other movements would improve as well! If she were not so afraid of being "soft" or vulnerable (Tin Man), her Lion would be direct without being disrespectful and her Scarecrow would be objective without being emotionally disconnected. You see, integrating the positive aspects of Tin Man would augment the other two in a dynamically positive manner.

I call it *working the triad* because, for each person, the missing movement changes over time and contexts. In one situation the missing movement might be Lion, and at another time it might be Scarecrow, and in another context it might be Tin Man. Thus, the growing and changing person is constantly working the Interpersonal Triad. As a result the companions begin to function intrinsically more and more like a whole.

Repeatedly I have witnessed this process work for people in all sorts of situations and roles. I've seen it help CEO's effectively navigate through serious interpersonal challenges as well as guide young children through schoolyard conflicts. I am confident that it will help you as well in any and all of your important relationship challenges. And if practiced over time, these principles will help you grow and mature, even as Dorothy changed through her journey along the Yellow Brick Road.

About the Author

Sam Alibrando was born and raised in a large Italian-American extended family in the Northeastern United States. His own yellow brick road took him through Rutgers University, where he received his BA in Psychology. He went on to the Chicago area, where he earned his MA in Counseling Psychology at Trinity University, and finally to Southern California to receive a second Master's degree and a Ph.D. in Psychology at Rosemead School of Psychology.

For nearly thirty years he has worked to help individuals and organizations mature and grow. He is a respected Southern California clinical psychologist and organizational consultant, working with organizations and senior executives coping with critical business and change management challenges. In addition to his clinical practice, he also has experience in executive assessment and development, executive coaching, team building, personnel selection and organizational development.

Sam has worked with executives at the American Red Cross, American Water States, Amgen, Cigna Healthcare, Coca Cola Bottling, Diversified Maintenance Service, Farmers Insurance, and other smaller firms in numerous organizations on a range of assignments all focused on diminishing conflict, enhancing communication and accelerating sound decision-making, especially in the wake of a business transition.

Sam is a frequent lecturer and seminar leader. His favorite topics include leadership development, managing difficult people, helping couples grow, addiction recovery, and how people change. In addition to his writing and speaking, he has served as Director of Fuller Psychological and Family Services and as an adjunct clinical professor at Fuller Graduate School of Psychology. He served as President of the San Gabriel Valley Psychological Association and liaison in government affairs to the California Psychological Association.

You can contact the author at www.yellowbrickroad-book.com.

0-595-42285-3
978-0-595-42285-2

CPSIA information can be obtained at www.ICGtesting.com
Printed in the USA
BVOW031056051011

272815BV00002B/1/A